Library of
Davidson College

APRA AND THE DEMOCRATIC CHALLENGE IN PERU

edited by
**EUGENIO CHANG-RODRIGUEZ
& RONALD G. HELLMAN**

BILDNER CENTER FOR WESTERN HEMISPHERE STUDIES

APRA

AND THE

DEMOCRATIC CHALLENGE

IN PERU

APRA AND THE DEMOCRATIC CHALLENGE IN PERU

Edited by
Eugenio Chang-Rodríguez
and
Ronald G. Hellman

Bildner Center for Western Hemisphere Studies

The Graduate School and University Center of
The City University of New York

This volume, and the seminar from which it is drawn, were sponsored by the Tinker Foundation Incorporated.

Copyright 1988 by
Eugenio Chang-Rodríguez and Ronald G. Hellman.

All rights reserved under International and Pan-American Copyright Conventions.
Published in the United States by the Bildner Center for Western Hemisphere Studies, New York.

Library of Congress Cataloging-in-Publication Data

APRA and the democratic challenge in Peru / edited by Eugenio Chang-Rodríguez and Ronald G. Hellman. -- 1st ed.
    p.   cm.
  Bibliography: p.
  1. Partido Aprista Peruano. 2. Peru--Politics and government--1871- I. Chang-Rodríguez, Eugenio. II. Hellman, Ronald G. III. Tinker   Foundation.
JL3498.A6A67 1988
324.285'07--dc19   88-8147
ISBN 0-929972-02-3

Cover:
Original photograph montage of Víctor Raúl Haya de la Torre by Teodoro Vega González. Printed with the permission of Eugenio Chang-Rodríguez.

Cover design by André Boucher.

Manufactured in the United States of America.
First Edition.

CONTENTS

Preface *vii*

Introduction
The Peruvian Aprista Party: A Historical Background *1*
Eugenio Chang-Rodríguez

The Aprista Generations and the Relations Between Government and Party in Today's Peru *15*
Luis Negreiros Criado

Foreign and Economic Policy and National Development *25*
César Atala Nazal

The Democratic Challenge in Peru *35*
Nicanor Mujica Alvarez Calderón

The Democratic Response to Terrorism *41*
Javier Valle Riestra

Nationalism and Social Integration *49*
Grover Pango Vildoso

The Parliament: Bulwark of the People's Power *57*
Luis Alva Castro

Origin and Diffusion of The Shining Path in Peru *65*
Eugenio Chang-Rodríguez

PREFACE

In June 1986, the Bildner Center for Western Hemisphere Studies convened a seminar on "The New Generation and the Democratic Challenge in Peru." This occurred toward the end of Alan García's first year as President of Peru. His party had also won a majority in both legislative houses.

García's Peruvian Aprista Party (PAP) had assumed office at a time of deepening difficulties in Peru. International and national indebtedness, violence and terrorism, the growing drug trade and a large marginal population were among the problems facing the new government. García, who had great popular support, took immediate action on some of Peru's social and economic crises.

Some sectors of the international community reacted cautiously to the new Aprista government. In fact, García's debt management program (payments limited to ten percent of export earnings) caused great consternation in many world capitals and financial centers.

The PAP was in office for the first time; moreover, its government was led and in many cases administered by members of a new generation. In the hope that some part of bilateral misapprehension could be allayed through closer contact, the Bildner Center invited U.S. leaders, scholars, journalists, and businesspeople to meet for two days with five high-ranking Aprista officeholders.

This book comprises the presentations that the Peruvian officials gave on six important areas of Peruvian domestic and international policy. Discussions and debates (not included here) followed the presentations; in this give-and-take, participants progressed from rhetoric and confrontation at the beginning of the seminar to frank and cooperative discussion by the end of the first day. It is difficult, of course, to measure "understanding," but the reactions of U.S. and Peruvian participants alike suggest that the seminar was successful.

Improving understanding among those involved in hemispheric affairs is an important goal of the Bildner Center. The Center sponsors research, forums, seminars, and publications that address the practical resolution of public policy problems in an increasingly interdependent world. It promotes increased collaboration among the faculties within The City University of New York (CUNY), and serves as a link between CUNY's intellectual community and other experts and policymakers working on contemporary issues in Latin America, the United States and the Caribbean. The Center provides a "window" on New York for scholars and public officials throughout the Americas. It is named for Albert Bildner, a philanthropist with extensive experience in hemispheric affairs.

In the spirit of providing a "window," and to provoke further discussion and debate, we are pleased to publish this volume of papers by the García government's representatives from both the executive and legislative branches. Views expressed in Bildner Center publications are the authors' and are not necessarily shared by those associated with the center or the CUNY Graduate School.

The Bildner Center is grateful to Professor Eugenio Chang-Rodríguez for the role he has played in this project and his contributions to this volume. His essays, including an introductory historical background to the first APRA government, draw upon his long experience as a scholar of Peruvian politics and his close ties to APRA and its leaders.

We also express our gratitude to Nicanor Mujica Alvarez Calderón, Minister of the Presidency, and Senator Armando Villanueva del Campo for their special cooperation in this project.

We would like to thank the Tinker Foundation Incorporated for funding the seminar and this publication. The Tinker Foundation focuses on Mexico, Central America, South America and Iberia within the broad areas of social sciences, international relations and natural resources.

Bildner Center Publications

Ronald G. Hellman
General Editor

Sheila Klee
Managing Editor

Julio Chan-Sánchez
Editorial Research

Introduction
the Peruvian Aprista Party:
A Historical Background

EUGENIO CHANG-RODRIGUEZ
Queens College of The City University of New York

PERUVIAN POLITICAL PARTIES BEFORE APRA

In Peru, the idea of founding a modern political party with appeal to the masses had been in the mind of many intellectuals and labor leaders since the middle of the nineteenth century. However, the country did not have a political mass movement before the emergence of the Peruvian Aprista Party (PAP)[1] in 1930. Before that year most political parties established in Peru were built around an individual leader (*caudillo*), in response to a group's special interests, without a well-sustained ideology, and lacking popular support.

The Civil Party (*Partido Civil*), founded in 1871 by the oligarch Manuel Pardo, was the first political party of the land. It was organized as a reaction against the rampant militarism that dominated Latin America. Although the *Civilistas* advocated the reduction of the standing army, they wooed the armed forces and chose General Mariano Ignacio Prado as their presidential candidate in the 1876 elections. Later, in 1886, they gave their calculated support to another general who aspired to the presidential office: Andrés Avelino Cáceres.

---

[1] "APRA" and "Aprismo" refer to the international movement founded in 1924. The Peruvian Aprista Party (PAP) is an APRA organization at the national level. Because Peru is the only country with an organized APRA party, the PAP is sometimes called "Aprismo" or "APRA".

The *Civilista* golden years were during the first two decades of this century, during which José Pardo y Barreda, Manuel Pardo's son, was elected president twice (1904-1908 and 1915-1919), before and after the administration of his minister of finance, Augusto B. Leguía. Leguía split the Civil Party and returned to power in 1919 to rule the country for eleven years. During these years he broke away completely from traditional *Civilismo* and, once he was consolidated in power, governed autocratically and exiled his political enemies, including the members of the APRA movement. After Leguía's downfall in 1930, the *Civilistas* attempted to make a comeback, but new forces were prominent on the political scene. Some *Civilistas* established the Decentralist Party and others joined Commander Luis M. Sánchez Cerro's Revolutionary Union. When Manuel Prado, the son of General Mariano Ignacio Prado, became president as General Oscar R. Benavides' political heir in 1939, the Civil Party was largely a thing of the past. Its members were scattered among the existing anti-APRA political forces.

The other political parties, which at times competed with the Civil Party and other times collaborated with it, were personalist and relatively insignificant. General Andrés Avelino Cáceres' partisans, for instance, founded the Constitutionalist Party in 1884. It was mainly the general's personal vehicle. He was elected president by his party and the *Civilistas* in 1886. Cáceres imposed Colonel Remigio Morales Bermúdez as his successor, who governed from 1890 until his death in 1894. Cáceres then imposed Colonel Justiniano Borgoño as president, but one year later an uprising led by the *Civilistas* and the Democratic Party ousted the Constitutionalist Party regime. Although Cáceres lived for almost thirty years more, his party never played a major role after 1894.

The Democratic Party was also organized in 1884 by Nicolás de Piérola, who first served as minister of finance under President José Balta from 1872 to 1876. In 1895 the Democratic Party formed an alliance with the Civil Party to mount a revolt against President Borgoño. After the victorious civil war, Piérola became president. In 1895 Piérola honored the commitment of his alliance and let the *Civilista* Eduardo López de Romaña assume the presidency. The Democratic Party never returned to power. It disappeared by 1920.

The Liberal Party was founded in 1900 by Augusto Durand. In 1912 it supported the candidacy of Guillermo Billinghurst, a populist-oriented millionaire. However, two years later, the Liberals joined forces with other groups to bring about the ouster of Billinghurst. Durand hoped to become president thereupon, but when this did not happen, the Democrats joined forces with José Pardo's branch of the Civil Party. The Liberal Party was disbanded after Durand's death in 1923 (Chang-Rodríguez 1982:591-94).

The last significant party prior to the appearance of Aprismo to be mentioned is the National Union. This was also a small political organization, made up primarily of liberal intellectuals of upper- and middle-class origin. It was organized in 1891 by Manuel González Prada (1844-1918) with the members of the *Círculo Literario*, an association of positivist writers founded by Luis E. Márquez in 1886. The Declaration of Principles of the National Union, written by González Prada, favored the federal form of government, mandatory minority representation in Congress, return of land to the Indian communities, substitution of the army by militias, and universal suffrage even for alien residents. Reflecting positivist philosophy, it favored European immigration and opposed that from Asia.

González Prada's sojourn in Europe between 1891 and 1898 weakened the party's effectiveness as an opposition party. *Germinal*, its main periodical, appeared on 1 January 1899, but a few weeks later it was closed down by the government. It reappeared in 1901 when some of the National Union's leaders began to support the Liberal Party which then had government connections. González Prada resigned from the National Union in protest. A few years later the party died out through inactivity.

THE POPULAR REVOLUTIONARY ALLIANCE OF AMERICA (APRA)

During the period of unrest unleashed in Latin America by the First World War the future founders of the APRA movement began their preliminary work in Trujillo, Peru. Initially they were a group of liberal intellectuals, some of them descendants of impoverished aristocratic families who were unable to cope with the expansion of neighboring hacienda *Casa Grande*, one of the world's largest sugar plantations; others were middle class university students and professionals. By 1915 all of them were writers and artists who participated in cultural activities and studied the causes behind the economic and cultural backwardness of Peru. Among the most prominent were Antenor Orrego, Víctor Raúl Haya de la Torre (1895-1979), César Vallejo, Alcides Spelucín, Carlos Manuel Cox, and Manuel Vásquez Díaz, joined later by Ciro Alegría.

In Lima, Haya de la Torre organized an alliance of workers and intellectuals as advocated by Manuel González Prada, one of the most popular writers of the country, whose political essays clearly excoriated corruption, injustice, and malign neglect on the part of the ruling alliance of oligarchs and militarists. This united front was able to secure an eight-hour work day, organize labor unions, and initiate the university reform, following the example set by the students of the University of Córdoba in Argentina in 1918. Under Haya's leadership, the National Congress of Students was convened in Cuzco in 1920, and shortly afterward the González Prada People's Universities (*Universidades Populares González Prada*) were founded to educate the workers on an open admission and free tuition program.

Haya was imprisoned and then deported in October 1923. Other student leaders were also jailed and exiled. Convinced by then that education alone could not reform their country, the young Peruvian leaders decided to turn to organized political action. In response to this demand, Haya de la Torre founded the American Popular Revolutionary Alliance (*Alianza Popular Revolucionaria Americana*, APRA) in Mexico City on 7 May 1924[2]. *The Labour Monthly*, the official organ of the Labour Party of England, published Haya's article "What's the APRA?" in its December 1926 issue. There Haya summarized the "maximum program" of the APRA movement, which stressed the political union of Latin America and the solidarity with all peoples and oppressed classes of the world. An intense campaign in Peru, with the aid of José Carlos Mariátegui (1894-1930) and his journal *Amauta*, and among the Peruvian students in Europe and the Americas, helped the growth of Aprismo. By 1929 there were APRA committees in Paris, Buenos Aires, Mexico City, Havana, New York, and other cities of Central America. The development of APRA as an international ideology has its roots in the intensive work accomplished by the different APRA cells in Europe and the Americas, and the publications by their members, particularly Haya de la Torre's articles and first books, outstanding among them *La emancipación de América Latina* and *El antiimperialismo y el APRA*.

---

[2] Most historians claim that the American Popular Revolutionary Alliance was founded in Mexico City on 7 May 1924 (Pike 1986:50). On that day Víctor Raúl Haya de la Torre (1895-1979) delivered the APRA flag of the "new Spanish-American generation" to the Federation of Mexican Students and explained that the flag's broad red field symbolized the new generation's "palpitating aspiration for justice", and its central golden map of Latin America, which he called Indoamerica, was mankind's haven (Haya 1977:2.7-8). Some anti-APRA writers conjecture that APRA was born at the end of 1926 or the beginning of 1927 when Haya established the Paris cell of the movement (Cf. Valderrama 1980:9 and Planas 1986:23-24).

THE PERUVIAN APRISTA PARTY (PAP)

The overthrow of President Augusto B. Leguía on 24 August 1930 paved the way for the founding of the the Peruvian Aprista Party the following September 20[3]. Alcides Spelucín gathered the APRA members coming out from prison and returning from exile. The arrival of Carlos Manuel Cox, Manuel Seoane, and Serafín Delmar strengthened the recently founded PAP and helped in converting it to the first political party of the country in the true sense of the word.

Aprismo is more than a political party. It is an ideological movement that has philosophical, political, economic, and educational manifestations[4]. Its intellectual framework rests on Haya de la Torre's thesis of historical space-time. After observing that philosophies of history and political philosophies have been traditionally linked to prevailing scientific knowledge, Haya de la Torre worked out his own interpretation of historical events, using Einstein's theory of relativity and Toynbee's conception of the perspective of the historian. Haya interpreted history as a vast universal coordination of processes, each one inseparable from its own space, time, and motion. The ingredients of his new term are historical space and historical time. Historical space, to him, is not only geographical space; it is also the relation of space to the social group as a living and thinking body that develops its group consciousness; it is the sum total of the geography of man, his ethnic composition, and the interrelation of these with the social consciousness.

Historical time, on the other hand, is not a chronological concept; it is the intuitive time that a social group senses as flowing from all the relationships between man as a part of the social group and his historical space. These two ingredients are inseparable. Each historical space determines the time and velocity of the development of the social institutions of the group, while the social consciousness of historical space determines the tempo of its culture. Thus, in this new concept, Haya de la Torre includes everything that affects the life of a social group.

Aprismo sees the world divided into continental peoples

---

[3] Most Apristas give this date (Sánchez 1978:195-98). My examination of the founding document and the testimony of some APRA leaders lead me to believe that the correct date should be 21 September 1930, inasmuch as the signing of the founding act took place after 12 p.m. of 20 September 1930, the day the founding meeting began (Cf. Chang-Rodríguez 1987:121).

[4] For Fredrick B. Pike, a well-known American historian, APRA is "more like a religious movement than a party" (Pike 1986:7).

(*pueblos-continentes*), some of which already constitute continental countries, such as the United States, China, the Soviet Union, India, and Australia. There are others, such as Indoamerica and the Arab world, which have not formed a single political state (Orrego 1939). For Haya, there is in each continental people a certain innate rhythm determined by the collective consciousness of their historical space-time, which in turn helps to determine their particular development along certain lines, despite the social institutions and ideological pressures from other continental nations. It is for this reason that the Apristas maintain that Latin America cannot adopt *prima facie* any European economic or political system developed in response to a European historical space-time. Latin America must work out a completely new system of government and economic organization, since capitalism, communism, and fascism, as developed thus far, are not suitable to present Latin American historical space-time.

The Apristas have two political programs: the "maximum program," applicable to all of Latin America, and the "minimum program," for each country according to its particular needs. The first is a long-range platform aimed at the creation of a democratic and powerful United States of Indoamerica, with appropriate institutions for the building and maintenance of its *pueblo-continente*.

The PAP's minimum program serves as an example of a domestic platform. It proposes an economic organization of Peru after setting up an economic congress and a national financial corporation. The economic congress would be formed by the representatives of nationals and foreigners participating in the country's economy: labor, management, government, and the professions. It would be an advisory agency in charge of economic planning. The national financial corporation would carry out the projects suggested by the economic congress and adopted by the regular political organs of the state. Other PAP ideas include administrative decentralization, a new geographic division according to an economic criterion, and the organization of producer and consumer cooperatives. An important item in the PAP's minimum program is the incorporation of the Indian population into the modern state. It aims to redeem Indians from bondage, undernourishment, illiteracy, impoverishment, not because they are Indians, but because they are exploited and marginalized citizens. Aprismo claims it does not make any racial distinctions.

PAP'S ELEVEN QUINQUENNIA IN WAITING

Haya de la Torre was the PAP's presidential candidate in the 1931 general elections. He was then 35 years old, the minimum constitutional age to run for that office. Fraud kept him from reaching the presidency, but twenty-two of his disciples were elected to the Constituent Assembly[5]. General Luis M. Sánchez Cerro, President of the Republic by virtue of the fraudulent vote count, expelled the Aprista representatives from the Assembly and outlawed their party in 1932. Several revolts to overthrow the dictator failed. The government launched a campaign of terror: thousands of Apristas were jailed and killed. Haya de la Torre was captured and placed in solitary confinement. He was saved from death by telegrams and letters of protest from important world personalities. After the assassination of Sánchez Cerro in 1933, General Oscar R. Benavides was imposed as his successor. While he consolidated his power, Benavides permitted the Apristas to exercise their constitutional rights, but after feeling himself secure in the presidency and in complete control of the country in 1934, he outlawed the Aprista Party and jailed and exiled thousands of its members. Scores of Apristas died in prison, the torture chambers, or while resisting arrest.

The PAP remained underground until 1945 when it was allowed to join the Democratic National Front (*Frente Democrático Nacional*) and was permitted to elect some senators and a majority in the Chamber of Deputies. Relations between the Apristas and José Luis Bustamante y Rivero, the President they helped to elect, soon became strained. He used the pretext of the naval revolt of October 1948 to outlaw the PAP. Without a solid and wide popular base, Bustamante was soon overthrown by his former minister, General Manuel A. Odría. During his entire dictatorship, from 1948 to 1956, Odría persecuted the Apristas with more intensity than his dictatorial predecessors had.

Banned from running for public office, the Apristas had no choice but to vote in 1956 for Manuel Prado, the only candidate who promised to restore civil liberties and political rights. Prado won the presidential elections and immediately after inauguration he repealed the exclusion laws, opened the prisons, allowed exiles to return, and permitted free political activities. During Prado's second term in office, from 1956 to 1962, the PAP reorganized its ranks and participated in the 1962 general elections. Although Haya de la Torre obtained more votes than any other candidates, the electoral board announced that the PAP's presidential candidate had obtained 32.94% of the votes, slightly less than the one-third required by law to win.

---

[5] The official results of the 12 October 1931 elections gave Sánchez Cerro 50.75% and Haya 35.38% of the votes (Rocangliolo 1980:25-28).

Obviously it was a repetition of the old story: a fraudulent vote count. As the ultimate decision rested with Congress, the APRA leaders approached Popular Action (*Acción Popular*) for an understanding. When Fernando Belaunde, its founder and top leader, rejected the offer, the PAP reached an understanding with the Odriísta National Union *(Unión Nacional Odriísta)* to break the impasse (Ortiz de Zevallos 1976:295). The armed forces thereupon revolted and installed a military junta, and called for new elections.

In the 1963 general elections, Haya was recognized to have received 34.36%. Belaunde, aided by the Communists, radical leftists, and Christian Democrats, received 39.05% of the votes and was declared the winner. During Belaunde's first term in office the Aprista Party and the National Odriísta Union were able to control both houses of Congress. The decision by the PAP leadership to collaborate with their former enemies unleashed a crisis in the rank and file of the party. Some leaders left the party and quite a few dissidents formed Rebellious APRA (*APRA Rebelde*), and some of them led the 1965 guerrilla movement (De la Puente 1976). Books and articles were written to criticize what their authors called APRA's abandonment of its revolutionary ideology and praxis. In 1968, just before the approaching elections, Belaunde was ousted. He repeatedly claimed that the military did not revolt against him as much as against the Apristas, who had been predicted to win in the scheduled 1969 elections.

The Revolutionary Government of the Armed Forces, first presided over by General Juan Velasco Alvarado from 1968-1975, and later by General Francisco Morales Bermúdez from 1975-1980, adopted some of the reforms advocated by the PAP, but remained adamantly opposed to the idea of allowing an Aprista electoral victory. Nevertheless, in the 1978 elections for the Constituent Assembly, the PAP emerged with the highest number of votes, 35.34%, and Haya with the highest number of preferential votes. The founder of Aprismo was elected president of the Constituent Assembly. On 2 August 1979, a few days after he signed the new Peruvian Constitution, he died.

The 1980 general elections gave a surprising triumph to Belaunde with 1,870,864 votes. The official results showed that Armando Villanueva, the Aprista presidential candidate, had received 1,129,991 votes. Of the total of 5,307,465 votes cast, 775,423 were voided and 408,244 were declared blanks. The National Electoral Board proclaimed eighteen Apristas elected to the 61-member Senate, and 58 Apristas elected to the 180-member Chamber of Deputies. Notwithstanding the official results, the PAP was still the single largest party in the country, because the votes for Belaunde were cast by a coalition of anti-Aprista and anti-militarist voters affiliated with the extreme leftist parties, the Christian Popular Party, and independents, in addition to the members and sympathizers of Belaunde's Popular Action Party.

PAP'S VICTORY AFTER HAYA'S DEATH

Before the founder of Aprismo died, he predicted that Aprista victory would come after his death. His optimism and hope became a reality on 14 April 1985. In the general elections of that day the PAP obtained 53.10% of the valid votes, more than the combined vote of all the other parties. United Left (*Izquierda Unida*), the coalition of Marxist parties that included the Socialist Revolutionary Party (*Partido Socialista Revolucionario, PSR*), received 21.25% of the votes, the second highest. The Christian Popular Party allied to the Movement of Haya Bases (*Movimiento de Bases Hayistas*) received 12% and Belaunde's Popular Action won only 6%. The rest of the participating parties received less than 1%, including General Francisco Morales Bermúdez's Democratic Front of National Unity (*Frente Democrático de Unidad Nacional*).

There is no question that the architect of the Aprista victory was its presidential candidate Alan García Pérez. Son of Carlos García Ronceros and Nytha Pérez de García, both important PAP leaders and descendants themselves of Aprista families, Alan García was born on 23 May 1949. His father, PAP's national organization secretary, was in jail during the first five years of Alan's life. During his high school years at José María Eguren National School in the Lima district of Barranco, Alan joined the PAP. In 1962 he met Haya de la Torre. Henceforth his life was to be decisively influenced by the founder of APRA. In 1965 he entered the Catholic University of Lima as a student of liberal arts and law. There he met some of the most important young members of the Christian Democratic Party, who would later become national leaders of several Marxist political organizations. He transferred to the University of San Marcos, from which he received his law degree in 1973.

Shortly after becoming a lawyer, Alan enrolled at the Complutense University of Madrid, where he was awarded a doctorate of law after successfully defending his thesis on "The Hierarchical Constitutional Conception of Society and Constitutional Law in the Independence of Spanish America." His thesis director was Manuel Fraga Iribarne. From Madrid he moved on to Paris to study sociology at the

Sorbonne and at the Institute of Higher Latin American Studies. To balance his budget, Alan turned to guitar playing and singing Latin American songs at a restaurant. In 1977, after beginning his research for his thesis on "Studies of Electoral Sociology and the History of the Peruvian Aprista Party," with the advisory assistance of François Bourricaud, he returned to Lima to resume his party political activities.

After accepting a teaching position at the National University Federico Villareal, Alan was elected the PAP's national organization secretary. In 1978 he was elected to the Constituent Assembly. Two years later, at the head of the Aprista list for candidates for the Chamber of Deputies, he was elected with a very high number of preferential votes after leading a vigorous campaign for Armando Villanueva, PAP's presidential candidate. In September 1982 he published his book *El futuro diferente: la tarea histórica del APRA*. There he re-examines the essential principles of Aprismo, relative to its coherence via the contributions of Hegel, Marx, and the Libertarians. He discusses Haya's contributions, offers a synthesis of Peruvian economic development of the present century, analyzes the present situation of the country, and suggests Aprista solutions of decentralization, cooperativism, and continental integration, the implementation of which will foster another kind of future. Alan reiterates Aprista interest in the simultaneous attainment of physical well-being and the respect for human rights, or, in the language of Haya, "bread with freedom" (*Pan con Libertad*) (García:1982).

Late in 1982, after the publication of his book, Alan García was elected Secretary General of his party: his bid for the presidency was assured. He was elected his party's candidate for the presidency of the nation in 1984. His campaign was carefully designed, but he also moved cautiously. As *The New York Times*'s correspondent in South America observed, he adopted "Haya de la Torre's gestures, intonation, even his habit of dressing soberly" (Riding 1985:3). Repeating his slogan "My commitment is to all Peruvians," his victory was a landslide.

Upon taking office on 28 July 1985, Alan García became the youngest elected president in the history of Peru and one of the youngest constitutional rulers in the world. During his first ten months in office, Alan García's administration set in motion a program of action to cope with the economic crisis, the worst in Peru's history, and other serious challenges to democracy.

The number of Mirage 2000 jets ordered from France by the Belaunde administration was reduced at the same time that a proposal was made to freeze the regional purchase of armaments. García initiated an economic program to check inflation by controlling prices, limiting government expenditures, lowering the rate of interest, and setting multiple exchange rates with the dollar. An intense anti-corruption campaign was launched. The new government began to reorganize the police with the dismissal of 37 generals for their engagement in corruption or their failure to perform their duties. It dealt crushing blows to the drug traffic mafias. Deep in the jungle the government forces assaulted the largest drug trafficking complex discovered thus far in Latin America, which consisted of sophisticated laboratories for the preparation of cocaine hydrochlorate, a network of illegal airports, modern communication equipment, and light aircraft furnished with computerized gear for landings and take-offs in areas of dense vegetation and changing atmospheric conditions.

One of the most controversial policies set in motion by Alan García was his decision to allocate an amount of no more than ten per cent of the total proceeds from Peruvian exports to servicing the foreign debt. This bold decision raised the eyebrows of the creditors even though Belaunde had already ceased payment of the interest on the fourteen billion dollars owed to foreign governments and banks. This unilateral decision generated intense debate abroad and made many reflect upon the burdensome problem of the foreign debt and the way it has become the major destabilizing factor of both the economy and the society of the developing countries.

At this important point in the political development of Peru, after García's first 10 months in office, the Bildner Center for Western Hemisphere Studies convened a seminar to bring together Peruvian and U.S. leaders, scholars, and businesspeople to discuss policy options facing the government in Lima. The following chapters are the presentations made at the time by five high-level members of the Peruvian government as well as the speech of Luis Alva Castro upon assuming the presidency of the Chamber of Deputies on 28 July 1987. These presentations and the essay on the Communist Party of Peru called Shining Path cover in greater depth many of the issues raised in this brief historical background.

In closing, Ronald G. Hellman and I would like to express our gratitude to the Bildner Center staff for their assistance at the different stages of the preparation of this volume and to the Tinker Foundation for its support of the entire project.

REFERENCES

Chang-Rodríguez, Eugenio
  1982   "Peru," in *Political Parties of the Americas*, ed. Robert J. Alexander. West Port, Conn.: Greenwood Press. Pp. 586-610.
  1987   *Opciones políticas peruanas*. 2nd ed. Trujillo: Editorial Normas Legales.

De la Puente, Luis
  1976   *El camino de la revolución*. Lima: Ediciones "Voz Rebelde."

García, Alan
  1982   *El futuro diferente: la tarea histórica del APRA*. Lima: n. p.

Haya de la Torre, Víctor Raúl
  1977   *Obras completas*. 7 vols. Lima: Juan Mejía Baca.

Orrego, Antenor
  1939   *El pueblo-continente. Ensayos para una interpretación de América Latina*. Santiago, Chile: Editorial Ercilla.

Ortiz de Zevallos, Javier
  1976   *La democracia peruana presenta pruebas*. Lima: Grafital.

Pike, Fredrick B.
  1986   *The Politics of the Miraculous in Peru: Haya de la Torre and the Spiritualist Tradition*. Lincoln and London: University of Nebraska Press.

Planas, Pedro
  1986   *Los orígenes del APRA: el joven Haya*. Lima: Okura Editores.

Riding, Alan
  1985   "Peru Puts Democracy to the Test," *The Lima Times* 533 (July 26):3-4.

Roncagliolo, Rafael
1980 *¿Quién ganó? Elecciones 1931-80.* Lima: DESCO.

Valderrama, Mariano, et al.
1980 *El APRA: un camino de esperanzas y frustraciones.* Lima: Ediciones "El Gallo Rojo."

The Aprista Generations and the Relations Between Government and Party in Today's Peru

LUIS NEGREIROS CRIADO
President of the Chamber of Deputies (1985-1986)
Co-Secretary General of the Peruvian Aprista Party (1985-1988)

I have gladly accepted this invitation to discuss, as a politician, some important aspects of contemporary Peru. I am not a scholar but a labor union leader who is in charge of the Presidency of the Chamber of Deputies of Peru. This is the first time in the history of the Peruvian Republic, which began in 1821, that a blue-collar worker has held the presidency of one of the three branches of our government. This fact illustrates the present reality of my country.

The United States has maintained, throughout its history, a very useful relationship with Peru. I am talking of the people of the United States, its founders, its great thinkers such as Jefferson, its leaders such as Washington and Lincoln, its poets such as Whitman. Peruvian emancipation was achieved, to a certain extent, with the help of the American people.

I am in this university to speak as any Peruvian politician should speak today: with sincerity, seriousness, and the confidence that we have something new to say. If new ideas were not discussed in a university, it would not be a university.

PARTY UNITY

Aprismo is the oldest political movement in Peru. It was founded in 1924. Socialist and communist organizations were founded earlier but did not achieve party-hood until the 1930s; and only in the 1970s did they achieve any importance.

This political movement, through the Peruvian Aprista Party (PAP), succeeded in electing our thirty-six-year-old candidate, Dr. Alan García Pérez, as President of Peru in 1985. This raises a question: is there a generational rupture?

The answer is no. There is harmonious coordination and collaboration among the different Aprista generations. The President of the Republic is now 37 years old; the First Vice President, Luis Alberto Sánchez, is 86; the Second Vice President, Luis Alva Castro, is 42. The executive branch has coherence, cordiality, and above all efficiency.

Luis Alberto Sánchez is also the President of the Senate; and I am the President of the Chamber of Deputies. Two completely different generations control the two houses of the Congress, yet it functions with the highest imaginable coordination.

The cabinet too has generational coordination: Nicanor Mujica, Minister of the Presidency, is 73 years old; Luis Bedoya Vélez, Minister of Housing, is 63 years old; Abel Salinas, Minister of the Interior, is 55; Grover Pango, Minister of Education, 38; Remigio Morales Bermúdez, Minister of Agriculture, 38; Manuel Romero, Minister of Industry, Trade, Tourism, and Integration, 40; and Javier Tantaleán, Head of the Planning Institute with the rank of Minister, is 41. In financial organizations, public enterprises, Departmental Corporations, and municipalities there are Apristas who are 70 years old and others who are 25 years old.

How has APRA escaped generational conflicts and ruptures when other parties have not? There is a fundamental reason. The party, until 1979, was headed by Víctor Raúl Haya de la Torre, APRA's founder and leader. Haya was a great teacher. Throughout his life, he educated both leaders and rank-and-file party members with equal dedication. He knew how to maintain a constant equilibrium. He established as a principle that there were not old Apristas or young Apristas but only Apristas.

Our Central Committee (*Comité Ejecutivo Nacional, CEN*) created the Peruvian Aprista Youth (*Juventud Aprista Peruana, JAP*) for young Apristas; the Peruvian Aprista Children (*Chicos Apristas Peruanos, CHAP*), our children's organization; Aprista professional groups; labor unions; peasant and worker's organizations; and women's groups. In APRA, we can say proudly, there are neither generational nor gender problems. Women have had, earlier than in other parties, a leading role.

In a country divided by prejudices, which date from long ago, APRA has never had racial conflicts. We have always had leaders of all ethnic extractions working together. We have leaders and rank-and-file members of diverse religious faiths, and non-believers. We have people of different cultural levels and activities. We do not have conflicts because APRA is, above all, a United Front of Manual and Intellectual Workers (*Frente Unico de Trabajadores Manuales e Intelectuales*).

PARTY-GOVERNMENT RELATIONS

It is relatively easy for me to explain the relations between the party and the government. Peru is ruled by the 1979 Constitution. It was drafted by a Constituent Assembly elected by the people with Víctor Raúl Haya de la Torre as Assembly President. This Constitution, considered by some foreign scholars as the best in Latin America, reflects, to a great extent, the thinking of APRA's founder.

Article 68 of the Constitution says: "The political parties are expressions of democratic pluralism." Article 70 says: "The state does not give preferential treatment to any political party. It provides, to all parties, free access to all its means of social communication, in proportion to the results of the previous parliamentary elections."

There is, then, a clear, interdependent relationship between the Peruvian Aprista Party and the government, guided by absolute respect for the principle of political pluralism. The Peruvian government does not belong to a party; the government is in charge of a state in which all the parties, without exception, are legal, and all of them have access to power. In my country there are no people persecuted for their ideas and no political parties outlawed.

The Aprista Party fulfills the roles of social mobilization, government planning, support of administrative work through its ministers and technocrats, and ideological support through its theoreticians. Ours, a party with exemplary discipline, is also a watchdog against corruption or fraud and control of partisan activity, and a zealous guardian of the public money. APRA considers government an ethical exercise.

Because ours is a revolutionary party, relations with the government do not have the transitory interest of conquering an electoral clientele in order to stay in government. This has been demonstrated during this first year of Alan García's administration. The PAP does and says what it thinks necessary, independently of the response of the masses. We have forged a party for a transcendental mission and not for satisfying temporal interests.

There is a relationship between the government and the party which has an informative and consultative character, and another one characterized by criticism, self-criticism, and initiative, through the presence of state officials in the party's Political Commission, and National Commissions on Government Planning, education, peasantry, agrarian and labor issues and other areas.

The party as a mass mobilizing tool calls assemblies or demonstrations in support of government policies and cooperates, without excluding other movements, in tasks such as Popular Cooperation, literacy, and vaccination.

The relationship between party and government does not constrain the former. The party has its own sphere of action. It competes ideologically and politically with other parties in the labor unions, universities, and popular organizations as part of a process of social mobilization. The party's own tasks include helping the community and providing popular education. It has supported, since its founding, soup kitchens, medical centers, vocational academies, and the González Prada People's Universities. These universities were the seedbeds, in a poor and dependent country, for the university leaders, peasants, workers, and professionals who today are in power.

THE CHALLENGE

Now let me touch upon some of the problems the government, the party and the nation must confront together. A well-known Aprista leader said that Peru is experiencing its greatest crisis and that any interruption of its democracy will deepen this crisis and will compromise the future not only of the state but also of the nation itself.

A profound analysis of contemporary Peru is not necessary in order to conclude that one of the most salient characteristics of Peruvian society is the violence which encompasses almost all the spheres of life. The increase of insurgency and counterinsurgency, of urban and rural delinquency, the aggressive behavior of the citizens, the display of violence in mass media, all these have a common root: the endemic economic crisis. Historically violence is not typical of Peruvian society. On the contrary, it is a contemporary characteristic of the industrialized countries and also of the incorporation of the peripheral societies into the world system.

Shining Path's terrorism, land invasions, and drug traffic are the most notorious examples of the extreme violence that exists in Peru.

Every day we see attacks on private and public properties. We also see, through the mass media, the wave of kidnappings. Hundreds of Peruvians, civilians and military, have been killed by Shining Path's merciless attacks.

The Aprista government, not wanting to answer violence with violence, has announced that terrorism will be fought with the force of the law. In this way it shows its respect for human rights. We will also fight Shining Path with laws to change the socio-economic structures of the country, especially in the emergency zone.

Poverty, without doubt, is one of the factors that feeds violence. We have sectors who live in extreme poverty, whose degradation is exploited by those who want to create chaos. A study sponsored by the Friedrich Ebert Foundation concludes that poverty is not created by the lack of natural resources or global poverty, but is due to inequality. Peru not only has a low gross product per capita but also a very unequal distribution of this product. Even poorer countries, such as India, have a more equitable income distribution. We accept that unequal income distribution is a common fact in all countries, but this inequality is more acute in Peru than in other parts of the world. In Peru 40% of the population live in extreme poverty.

Data reveal that before the Alan García administration assumed office on 28 July 1985, wages and employment were rapidly decreasing. Poverty extended itself to the urban areas. Only one out of three Peruvians had a level of income that could be called adequate. In 1985, 56% of the economically active population and more than 60% of the employed people were under-employed, that is, they received incomes lower than the minimum subsistence level. Furthermore, unemployment was a reality for more than 700,000 Peruvians who were able to work. The capacity of the modern industrial sector to absorb the labor force was severely limited. In the last five years the number of unemployed has doubled and since 1972 it has quadrupled. On top of this, income levels have been at a record low.

REGIONALIZATION AND DEBUREAUCRATIZATION

Another important challenge to democracy in Peru is centralization and bureaucratization: 70% of the national product and 60% of the commercial, industrial, financial, and cultural activities are concentrated in Lima and Callao, as well as 27% of the population. This creates an asphyxiating centralism. The Aprista Party has proposed a decentralization process which the government is implementing. But the radicals try to thwart it by transforming it into a struggle of the countryside against the cities.

To solve the problem of centralism the productive forces of the regions must be developed. This can only be carried out by a mass political organization, such as the Aprista Party, and not by the official bureaucracy, no matter how efficient.

As happens in developing countries, Peru suffers from the negative consequences of over-bureaucratization. The state apparatus is oppressive and corrupt. This evil can only be eliminated by such a multi-class political organization as the PAP, with its teams of fully committed professionals imbued with a doctrine. This is a service that APRA provides to the present government.

President García's administration has already adopted several measures to solve the problem of over-bureaucratization and to decentralize state enterprises. Debureaucratization is achieved through a process aimed at the establishment of a new relation of confidence between those who govern and those who are governed, the reduction of redtape, the vitalization of the task of governing, the improvement of efficiency, and the moral renewal of society.

THE INTERNATIONAL DEBT

In addition to the challenges of violence, poverty, centralization, and bureaucracy, we face the challenge of the debt. On this issue, in his basic book *El antiimperialismo y el APRA*, Haya de la Torre said that anti-imperialist states will have to deal with imperialism because we need capital in order to reach the industrial development stage in our countries. For this reason APRA rejects the unilateral disavowal of the external debt. Our government has limited debt payments to 10% of export earnings. We honor our obligations, but we want to pay according to our ability.

Alan García stated in his speech to the United Nations General Assembly that under present conditions the external debt will not be satisfied by any of our countries because the effort would drown our democracies in misery and violence. The choice is dramatic: debt or democracy. Furthermore he has proposed a program to deal with the external debt, economic and technical cooperation, and peace in Central America.

Haya de la Torre once asserted that "the unity of our Latin American countries is the greatest guarantee against any imperialism and is the only effective way for development" and that just as the revolutionary struggle for political independence had to be transformed into a continental enterprise, our economic emancipation will also depend on the unity of all the Indoamerican people.

In more contemporary terms, Alan García, in his address to the

Peruvian nation in 1985, said that in the same way that all Peru was wholeheartedly supporting Argentina in the Malvinas conflict, the Americas must together support the example and actions of the Contadora Group in defense of Latin American sovereignty, which is being decided today in Central America, especially in Nicaragua.

DEMOCRATIC SOCIALISM

Since 1984, Peru's political spectrum has been polarized into two large forces: the PAP and the United Left (*Izquierda Unida, IU*), formed mainly by communists. The PAP maintains a plurality, but the IU represents an important second force, particularly in the municipal governments. In the Parliament, the United Left has 26% of the seats. In the municipal governments of the country the conservative parties are relatively insignificant while in Parliament they all together sum up 12%. In labor unions and universities IU members are a majority, followed by Apristas.

Recently, United Left opposition has increased in the form of mass mobilizations, stoppages, and strikes. The Parliament has been the scene of hunger strikes by radical members of both the Senate and the Chamber of Deputies, causing a confrontation between them and the police force. These activities are clearly of political character. They explain the confusion and desperation of these groups in reaction to the initiatives of the Aprista administration. At the regional level, and especially in the most depressed areas, the government, as never before, has doubled and tripled investments in infrastructure and health and education services. It has been applying, through microregionalization, policies aimed at reactivating the economic conditions, such as zero interest rate, minimum prices, and other measures.

The government maintains constant dialogue with peasant and base organizations. To date it has held three meetings, called *Rimanacuy*, in the north, center, and south of the country. The PAP is speaking to the people in their own language. The President of the Republic and the ministers go to peasant communities and speak in Quechua, which has never occurred before. (Quite a few radical politicians are bourgeois: they speak Spanish and English or French only.)

Haya said that the Communist Party is an exclusive class party, whose origins have been determined by European conditions, very different from ours, and whose political direction is determined in Moscow. Other Communist centers have been created more recently, but this does not change the essence of Haya's analysis. Aprismo is a revolutionary movement fighting for transformations of the Peruvian economy and society. But these changes have to be attained without falling into dictatorship which cancels freedom and human rights. We want deep and profound changes, but not in any way, not at any price, not at any time. Because of this, the PAP defines itself not only as a revolutionary organization, but also as a democratic party.

The PAP differs from the Communist Party in that it comprises exploited classes. It is a United Front of Manual and Intellectual Workers. It represents the interests of the rural working class, the blue collar industrial workers, and the middle class, which encompasses artisans, small merchants and small urban and rural entrepreneurs, professionals, and white collar workers. Haya stated that "Communism is the party of the proletariat class, whereas Aprismo is a party of productive classes threatened by the big monopolies of imperialist capitalism. Aprismo is a united front of classes within one party, with a common socio-economic program and a vigorous educational discipline." For Aprismo, Marxism is a historical philosophy which in America we would like to surpass in realism and devotion for the benefit of all, not only of the proletariat.

In Peru we are witnessing the resurgence of old polemics between Apristas and Communists. If APRA were to deny active support to the government, it would not only permit the hegemony of the United Left in the Parliament, but would also make possible forms of radical opposition which could frustrate the objectives and aims of the PAP's plans and programs.

APRA'S GOVERNMENT PLAN

To meet these challenges, the administration is trying to implement the PAP government plan, which reflects 70 years of study. The most salient aspects of this plan are:

1) To consolidate the democratic system, in order to create an economic and social democracy with wide and effective participation;

2) To dramatically modify the situation in the interior of the country; to give new value to the Andean culture; and to decentralize political decisions;

3) To strengthen the national identity; to create a new spirit of development, and to give confidence back to the Peruvian people;

4) To begin the transformation of the productive structure; to give priority to agriculture; to restructure industry; and to promote efficiency and productivity;

5) To modify patterns of savings and investments, of surplus accumulation and distribution; to increase national savings from 12% to 18% of the gross domestic product;

6) To consolidate an efficient and dynamic state which promotes and supports the national entrepreneur;

7) To integrally reform the educational system and to enable people to work and participate;

8) To develop a nationalist, independent and non-aligned foreign policy; and

9) To stop the deterioration and re-establish the balance of the ecological systems.

The success of the Aprista government plan is shown by the statements made, a few days ago, by the Minister of Economy and Finance, Luis Alva Castro: "In July 1985 the country was en route to hyperinflation that would have reached 250% or more. With the economic policy that we are applying, annualized inflation has been reduced to less than 70%. It is true that there was a seasonal price increase during the summer months (78% annualized). But inflation started to descend in April. Thus, in the last three months annualized inflation went down to 64% and during the month of May annualized inflation reached 48%."

Minister Alva Castro added that "Reactivation is only a step...the development of the national economy has other challenges." However, he also underlined that "There has been an increase in employment and in the purchasing power of all Peruvians."

Data supporting his assertions shows that GDP grew by 8.5% between April 1985 and April 1986, and some sectors have had record growth rates, such as fishing 172%, manufacturing 17%, construction 15.4%, and electricity 14.5%. At the same time, the inflation rate in May 1986, 3.3%, is one of the lowest in many years.

CONCLUDING REMARKS

1. The Peruvian Aprista Party does not practice a McCarthyist anticommunism that justifies oligarchical privileges or totalitarianism. We believe that Marxism is a valuable instrument for a better knowledge of the social problem, but we reject one-party totalitarianism, class struggle, and human rights violations.

2. The relations between the PAP and the present government are collaborative and interdependent. APRA is not subjugated to the government or vice versa.

3. APRA is respectful of the constitutional order and therefore of a multi-party system and public liberty. We fervently believe that only with public liberty and independent powers is it possible to transform the country.

4. The Aprista Party carries out its government plan through its

Aprista Parliamentary Committee (*Célula Parlamentaria Aprista*) and through the mayors and council members elected by the people.

5. The organs that control public functions, such as the Office of the Comptroller General, the Public Ministry, and the Judiciary, are in the charge of officials who are not Party members. They are appointed through the mechanisms established in the constitution in order to maintain their autonomy.

6. The party, as a United Front of Manual and Intellectual Workers, has a role of integrating classes, regions, and towns of the country.

7. The Aprista Party is an open organization, with offices throughout the country, with a permanent process of indoctrinization and proselytism to attract adherents.

8. Any Peruvian can be member of the party if he/she accepts its principles and its discipline; and any Aprista can leave the party without any problem.

9. We are a party in a constant process of affirmation and renovation, with a doctrine and a history, with a tactic and a strategy.

10. APRA maintains cordial relations with all legal organizations in Peru and others abroad. It is not a member of any international organization.

Foreign and Economic Policy and National Development

CESAR ATALA NAZAL
Ambassador to the United States
Former Minister of Industry, Trade, Tourism and Integration

FOREIGN POLICY

The foreign policy of the Alan García administration may not be readily understood or properly evaluated unless the ideological principles on which it has been based from the time of the APRA's founding in 1924 are clearly comprehended. These principles, defined in terms of nationalism, non-alignment, anti-imperialism and integration, sustain the program of action of the Peruvian Aprista Party's foreign policy. It is proper to mention at this point that all these tenets and the ideas expressed by President García, during the time since the Aprista Party assumed the offices of the government of Peru, are part of the Aprista ideology. There is absolutely nothing that this government has expressed from 28 July 1985 to this day that is not an integral part of the ideology of APRA as enunciated since 1927 and followed through the years under the guidance of its chief and founder, Víctor Raúl Haya de la Torre.

Nationalism in the Latin American/Indoamerican framework has to be analyzed and understood in a different context from the type of nationalism that prevailed in Europe prior to the First World War. That kind of restrictive nationalism has nothing to do with the Latin American nationalism embodied in the Aprista doctrine. When we speak about nationalism, we basically want to express the need to revive, strengthen, and put into proper focus the meaning and influence of the civilizations that existed in America prior to the arrival of the Spaniards and which have been for the most part neglected, abandoned, and even reneged upon.

The arrival of the Spaniards stopped the process of evolution of the Inca civilization quite effectively. This may not have happened by a malicious design of the Spanish Crown, but simply because the Spaniards were convinced, probably in good faith, that they were superior not only in the biological sense, but superior in the sense that their society had progressed immensely more than the Incas. And, more importantly, they were fanatically sure that the Christian God was the driving force of their actions and destiny. For the Spaniards, since the "pagan" Inca society was destined to fall inevitably to hell, Spanish Catholics had to show the way to salvation, even if this meant killing Indians.

The presence of the Spaniards, their technological superiority, weapons, and domination paralyzed the process of evolution of the Inca culture. And so it came about that the process of coexistence was not necessarily friendly at all times. It has been marked, more than by anything else, by the mutual distrust between the two cultures. This mistrust in many ways prevented real integration, a precondition for the development of a truly national consciousness in both segments. This situation prevails, to a certain extent, to this day.

Because I was born and educated through high school in a small village up in the Andes, I could go on speaking for hours about aspects of daily life in the highlands which show the devastating effects of the segregation that has marked the life of Peru since its conquest. One of the greatest merits of the Aprista movement, and this is what impressed me the most when I was a young boy, was its dedication to integrating Peru into a more modern society, based upon social and historical justice. To this day, the Peruvian Aprista Party (PAP) probably is the best example of the partial success in the integration that we are bent on achieving in Peru. Aprista citizens of Puerto Maldonado, a town in the jungle, and Aprista citizens of Piura, a city on the northern coastland, think very much alike of Peru as a nation. We have a vision of the country, a common vision we learned from the extraordinary teacher, Haya de la Torre.

That integrating process, nationalism, helps to explain, to my mind, something that we heard here this morning as possibly being divisive: generational differences within the party. I do not think there are any. In this seminar there are two Apristas of the older generation: Nicanor Mujica and myself; together we add up about one hundred years of Aprista history. The two of us used to work with the father of Luis Negreiros, the unforgettable Secretary General of the Aprista Party, killed in 1949 by General Manuel A. Odría's dictatorship. Between Mujica and myself and the Apristas of younger generations, I do not find any difference other than perhaps the color of our hair, or the lack of it.

Nationalism, as an internally integrating force, and Latin American continental nationalism, also a reinforcing integrating instrument, are part of the essence of APRA's ideology and, with the PAP in power now, a very important element of the Peruvian government program.

Non-alignment is the second principle. If we were looking for reasons for self-satisfaction as PAP members, we could consider that the idea of non-alignment started to evolve in Haya de la Torre's mind during the Anti-imperialist Congress held in Brussels in 1927. At that time there was a different world. The polarization we observe today between the two great superpowers did not then exist. Europe as a whole still was very powerful and the United States, after its participation in World War I, started to emerge as one of the most important powers in the world. The Soviet Union, on the other hand, was still getting out of one of its worse economic crises and hardly anybody would have thought at the time that it would become the other pole in this struggle that we are witnessing today. Yet Haya de la Torre declared that the Latin American countries should be aligned "neither with Washington nor with Moscow." This was a way of clearly defining the purpose of self-reliance in Indoamerica.

Today, you have one thousand different ways of interpreting non-alignment. For us, Apristas, it continues to be the best way of achieving self-reliance, of getting the necessary self-confidence for our own people's realization of our independent destiny. At the same time, it is a way to contribute to world peace. It would be a disservice to humanity if the Latin American countries aligned themselves with one or the other of the contending poles.

It is very important to keep in mind that for the Peruvian government and the Aprista Party the commitment to the democratic principles is an integral part of non-alignment. So it should be very clear that our non-alignment as well as our nationalism implies no hostility against anyone.

While I was Minister of Industry, Trade, Tourism, and Integration of Peru, I went to Moscow to renegotiate our debt with the Soviet Union. When I came back, I said half-jokingly that I wished Haya de la Torre were alive so I could ask him whether "with Washington and with Moscow," commercially and industrially speaking, would also be a form of non-alignment.

The third tenet of our ideological make-up is perhaps the most interesting. Its connotations are wide and deep, its misinterpretation is rampant and implications can very well be misleading. That is, anti-imperialism. I know of no thinker, of no political leader in Latin America who has analyzed and written about this phenomenon with more pragmatism, depth, and authority than Haya de la Torre. His understanding and teachings about imperialism were not motivated by the desire to exploit the benefits of propaganda coming out of the sounding boards provided by the extreme left everywhere.

In Latin America during the 1920s, when the Aprista party was founded, there was no way of avoiding an anti-imperialistic feeling and commitment. At that time, the United States occupied Nicaragua with marines and had an active intervention in the affairs of the Dominican Republic. The Platt Amendment was a daily and oppressive political reality in Cuba, the Panama Canal and the rest of the Republic of Panama were unabashed American reserves, and financial imperialism was rampant in Peru and elsewhere in the region.

It was Franklin D. Roosevelt, the great American president, who in the early 1930s inaugurated the Good Neighbor Policy, withdrew the American troops from Nicaragua, had the Platt Amendment repealed, and, generally speaking, gave all the indications of a dramatic change in U.S. foreign policy. Haya de la Torre and his Aprista Party were the first to recognize and welcome the change but insisted that, to be meaningful and credible, change had to be implemented through the support of the democratic form of government, as opposed to the coddling of local dictatorships in the hemisphere. Following this line of thinking, the action of the Aprista Party was coherent and true to its democratic substance when it aligned itself with the U.S. and its allies against the Axis Powers during the world conflict that started in 1939, at a time when the Apristas were attacked and persecuted by the dictatorship of General Oscar R. Benavides.

After the war, imperialism, while not totally absent from Latin America, took a different approach to obtaining economic benefits in the area. Anti-imperialists had to make every effort to correct the inequities in foreign investments and the enormously lopsided advantages usually offered and, fundamentally, to induce Latin American economic development in a broadly nationalistic context, that is, by making much wider opportunities possible for the nationals of each country in the region.

In the course of time, and largely because of the ever-changing adaptation of capital investment, the number of U.S. corporations operating in Latin America diminished considerably. As a matter of fact, when, a few weeks ago, I was invited to address the representatives of all the American corporations operating in Peru, I felt rather disappointed to see that there were so few of them present: one mining company, a couple of oil corporations, and the gentlemen representing firms engaged in selling detergents, chewing gum, and the like. Why so few? Is it that imperialism has disappeared from Peru? Not at all. It has changed once more. It is now expressed by its development and control of high technology.

The development of high technology probably has the redeeming features of enhancing knowledge and improving the conditions and circumstances of human societies. But its extremely high cost for poor countries like Peru make it inevitably, and even possibly without political design, the expression of modern imperialist power, firmly in the hands of highly industrialized countries including, of course, the Soviet Union. The financial implications of their control are certainly obvious. Therefore, the long-standing anti-imperialistic position of the Aprista Party, now in power in Peru, should by no means be interpreted as anti-American or anti-any other nationality.

Luis Negreiros' excellent presentation gives an overview of our position on economic and social development. I would like to stress what Negreiros said regarding foreign investments in Peru. Our anti-imperialism does not contradict our attitude toward foreign investments. We are in favor of all investments that really help the people of Peru, particularly the foreign investments that, while taking a fair share of the benefits, will clearly show that they are carried out with absolute respect for our laws and institutions and, first and foremost, that they are to the financial and social advantage of the host country as well.

Integration is the fourth Aprista principle on my agenda. Since its early days, APRA has held Latin American integration as one of its most important ideological tenets. An anti-imperialistic position, in order to bring a truly emancipating result, had to be sustained on a regional basis. Latin America, or Indoamerica as we call it, has to become a union of free countries, a single voice in international affairs. Apristas believe that sustained economic and social development is unattainable in national isolation, both from the political point of view and in regional economic interests. "The disunited countries of Latin America could not compete with the United States of America," to quote one of the graphic dictums of Haya de la Torre.

The day the first Aprista president, Alan García, took power in Peru on 28 July 1985, after winning one of the purest elections we have ever had, he made it very clear that Latin American integration was to be one of his most important concerns. Peru is now actively trying to help unify and strengthen the determination to defend and promote democracy as the best possible form of political organization throughout the region. Alan García, unilaterally and quite courageously, started a policy of disarmament and immediately began to implement it as a proof of his government's conviction that in Latin America we have no place or need for any military conflict.

In relation to the critical problem of the Latin American external debt, President García has also repeatedly asserted that it is a global problem, while establishing uniquely Peruvian ways to handle it. We are hoping against hope that both creditors and debtors will find the problem more tractable if dealt with on a global basis than in agonizing and counterproductive isolated ways.

The Peruvian Government is determined to help revive and inject more vitality into the subregional integration efforts, particularly the Andean Pact. It will try to find, under the common leadership of the other government members of the Pact, the reason for its sluggishness and then adopt whatever measures are required to make it work.

Contrary to superficial and rather stereotyped conclusions, I firmly believe that a better-defined and self confident Latin America, and certainly a popular, nationalistic, non-aligned and anti-imperialistic Peru, will be much more reliable friends of the United States than the countries in the past represented by the likes of Somoza, Duvalier, and others. It is in this context that Peru welcomes the new attitude of the present U.S. administration when it powerfully asserts its commitment to democracy everywhere. It is certainly one of the most encouraging facts of our time in the old and continuous struggle to help firmly establish democracy throughout Latin America and the Caribbean.

The Aprista Party, now in power in Peru, has long understood, however, that the promotion and establishment of political democracy, though of the highest priority, are not enough. We have to find ways and means for the democratic form of government to respond to a social and economic framework capable of providing opportunities for the common people and to be strictly determined to eradicate social injustice.

For that noble purpose we honestly believe there is no more efficient vehicle than a democratic, popular, non-aligned, and anti-imperialistic government for Peru. These political conditions in no way preclude better and sounder relations with this great country, the United States. To this we are also committed.

ECONOMIC POLICY

It is, of course, understandable that the international financial community is a bit uneasy about the declarations made by President García on the Peruvian external debt and, in general, on the economic program his government has instituted since August 1985. As a former member of the first cabinet of the García government and now as a representative of the Peruvian government in the United States, I will try to explain, and hopefully justify, our economic and financial policies of today.

It should be kept in mind that long before President García took over the government in July 1985, the previous Peruvian government had already discovered that it was unable to maintain the service of the Peruvian external debt. It is important, therefore, to realize that the García government found Peruvian finances in quite a tight spot and with no prospect of relief in sight. The decline of Peruvian exports, due mainly to the serious fall of the international price of its commodities, had begun in 1980 and the downward trend has remained constant to this date, an unusually long time. Peruvian foreign exchange revenues became insufficient to take care of debt obligations. Most of the debts had been contracted during the euphoria of the petrodollar allocations, creating, at some point, the illusion of prosperity forever. The cost-benefit relationship of projects and programs during the time of euphoria probably was calculated in a somewhat lopsided way.

Peru's economy, like those of many other Latin American countries, in the past followed the cycles of the industrialized world. That is to say, during this long cyclical period, the ups and downs of the Peruvian economy were dictated by the prices paid in the international markets for the commodities Peru exports, such as copper, silver, fishmeal, oil, and cotton.

For as long as the cyclical period prevailed, and considering that the ups followed the downs in relatively rapid succession, Peru had found a rather subdued and underdeveloped way of managing its economy and finances in an acceptable way from the international creditors' standpoint.

Times do change, however, and, temporarily at least, they have changed not exactly for the better. The technological revolution that the industrialized world is undergoing today, and suffering from and profiting by, has had a tremendous negative impact in the raw materials-producing countries like Peru. The technological revolution is probably the most important cause of the decline in the price of many export commodities. Take for instance the case of copper. Today, a telephone system could be installed in any city, be it New York, Tokyo or Lima, without the need of as much as a foot of copper wire. The technological revolution has provided cheaper substitutes readily available right in the industrialized countries. As a consequence, the international price of copper has fallen by more than half and, of course, so have the revenues coming from the export of copper.

In the case of silver something similar has occurred. The biggest industrial users of silver, mainly the manufacturers of photographic and x-ray films and computer chips, have found ways, through the technological improvement in recycling and substitution, to save to an extent to which the demand for silver has also been steadily going down. This in spite of the well known efforts of the Hunt Brothers to speculate on silver prices with rather catastrophic results, especially for the silver market.

The same thing has happened with other items of our export structure, including fishmeal, which has been replaced by soya beans. Even oil, the glamour export of golden times, is no longer the certain guarantee of substantial export income. It is not so much the OPEC policies, but the technologies of conservation and substitution, that have diminished the lion's share which this product used to enjoy.

President García's government, on its inauguration day, 28 July 1985, realized that it faced an extremely complex and difficult situation in the times ahead. Internally, inflation was virtually out of control and, what is worse, it existed within an environment of economic pessimism which made it appear as if inflation was almost unbeatable. Unemployment was extremely high and on the rise. Social pressures had been accumulating, frustration after frustration. And, finally, terrorism had increased in violence to the point at which the cost of fighting it threatened to consume a rather high proportion of the national budget.

In this situation, so briefly summarized, President García had to be creative and bold, energetic and persuasive in his determination to find some solutions to Peru's economic and financial problems. To take care of the immediate internal economic problems, above everything else, measures were needed to stop the inflationary psychosis. Before establishing price controls, open and careful negotiations were started between the government and the main industrialists and businessmen of Peru, so as to make them work on the basis of a national consensus. The importation of luxury products was drastically curtailed and a very vigorous effort to put the idle capacity of the industrial plant to work was set in motion. An income policy was readjusted so as to guarantee a better distribution of wealth and, obviously, to provide the Peruvian people with some immediate relief for their very depressed living conditions. The sense of participation of the poorer population in all aspects of national life was immediately stimulated. A growing, almost palpable faith in the government's programs and intentions ensued, encouraging national self-esteem and confidence. So far things seem to be working quite satisfactorily in Peru, as a good beginning.

On the external side of things, President García had to deal without delay with the external debt problem. After a very careful analysis of the financial position of Peru and its social and economic demands, he had no other choice than to make his announcement that Peru, while intent on paying its external debt, could not thereafter pay to its creditors more than the equivalent of ten per cent of its export earnings.

The García declaration on 28 July 1985 on the Peruvian external debt was fundamentally the acknowledgment of a fact coming neatly out of the Peruvian economic and financial situation of the moment. However, in some sectors of the international financial community, this declaration was interpreted as a sort of a challenge to the system. The vigorous and forceful rhetoric which this young and dedicated President used in his inaugural address might have encouraged some to believe that García's assertions were not based upon solid ground.

Peru is determined to pay its foreign debt and I have no doubts that it will do so. Peru will expect, however, that the creditor nations and institutions accept the limited payments coming out of the ten-percent-of-exports formula until such time as its foreign exchange income substantially increases and the immediate acute social and economic problems facing the Peruvian population show lasting signs of improvement. This would be one way, probably the only one, to maintain and strengthen the stability of a truly democratic government. The concept of shared responsibilities among creditor and debtor countries has to be acknowledged and sustained, not in the sense of guilt distribution, but with a clear view that the development of free and democratic nations is perhaps the major responsibility of Western Civilization at the present time.

The Democratic Challenge in Peru

NICANOR MUJICA ALVAREZ CALDERON
Minister of the Presidency (1985-1987)

The relationship between Anglo-Saxon America and Latin America (we Apristas prefer to call it Indoamerica) is of immense importance. It is of such importance that we can hardly overemphasize it. Unfortunately, ideas and writings of United States think-tanks and policymakers are increasingly difficult to obtain in Peru. Magazines that until recently were circulating in the Andes are now out of our reach due to economic strains. Meanwhile, totalitarian countries are flooding our republic with their publications, nicely printed, and at very low prices or for free. What we do get from the U.S. usually concerns American affairs, while publications coming from the East are aimed at the ideological conquest of vast social sectors, which, lacking a solid democratic preparation, fall into the trap. This infiltration is efficiently backed with many well-endowed scholarships for university studies, which seduce low-income people who want to achieve the better social status that the professional diploma confers.

Given this situation, we are especially pleased with this opportunity to exchange ideas with scholars and policymakers in the United States. The youthful Alan García Pérez, as the leader of the Peruvian Aprista Party (PAP), has begun a profound transformation in Peru and has also awakened both fears and sympathy elsewhere in the Americas. I suspect that this seminar's topic, "The New Generation and the Democratic Challenge in Peru," was proposed because of some doubts about the abilities of the young men who now have the Peruvian destiny in their hands.

To ease these doubts, consider the historical evolution of the PAP, whose ranks were constantly swelled by waves of youngsters. In Peru, as in the rest of the Americas, we are accustomed to speak of generations of intellectuals, scientists, and politicians, formed by groups of people with more or less coherent outlooks, outstanding in their fields, who attempt to interpret in their own way their generational feelings and thinking. Prior to Víctor Raúl Haya de la Torre's founding of APRA, there were several intellectual, scientific and political "generations" in Peru. Some historical examples are the generation which established the first civilian government in our republican period, headed by President Manuel Pardo in the 1870s; the generation of Manuel González Prada, the great rebel, anarchist, outstanding social critic, and poet; and the highly intellectual generation of a party branded *"Futurista,"* which had at its center José de la Riva Agüero. All these generations withered away. They occupy a historical period strictly defined by a few years and nothing more.

The scheme changes in 1920 with the advent of Haya de la Torre. The great thinker and leader remained vital and active from the time of the great social struggle of that epoch until a few weeks before he died in 1979. He personally trained politically successive waves of youngsters of middle class and working class origin. These disciples pursue his doctrine with slight interpretive variations while maintaining his solid ideological core. In his "Christmas Message to the Nation" (1932), written while confined in the Lima Penitentiary, where the Sheraton Hotel now stands, Haya said the young Apristas were an important complement to the leaders of his generation. When two years later he founded the Federation of Aprista Youth (Federación Aprista Juvenil, FAJ), Haya preferred to call it PAP's graduating class (*promoción*), initiated to assist the "founding generation of Aprismo," to which he, Manuel Seoane, Antenor Orrego, Carlos Manuel Cox, Manuel Vásquez Díaz, Luis Heysen, Luis Alberto Sánchez, and many more belonged.

APRA is the longest lasting political movement in the country. Víctor Raúl Haya de la Torre said that Aprismo is not dogmatic, closed or arbitrary, but a line of action to the infinite. The crew of the Aprista ship constantly receives reinforcements of new graduating classes who maintain the same course. As Kipling said, the game is more important than the men who play it; the ship is more valuable than the crew. We Apristas believe that we are all "*promociones*" within the same school of thought, rather than different generations within the movement. Each graduating class shares the same fundamental credo, but brings the natural influences of the different historical period in which it was formed.

Haya continued to educate new "*promociones*" until his final days in 1979, through his writing and his use of the Socratic colloquial method. Every week, in the Great Hall of the People *(Aula Magna de la Casa del Pueblo)*, thousands of people, coming from all the provinces of the country, gathered to hear him. He answered the questions of the wise and of the ignorant. He also used to meet with the advance guard of the youth in long meetings in his country house. From these training sessions emerged the present political leadership of the Aprista government. Among them, the best and the most original of his disciples is the young Alan García, who has now picked up the doctrinal torch, and, in the same *Aula Magna*, works directly, intellectually, and personally, with the Aprista youth.

Alan, as he is called with affection in Peru, is the son of a PAP leader who distinguished himself by his dedication to the party, his devotion to its cause, and his austere and stoic personal life during the worst years of our underground work imposed by the successive dictatorships. His mother was a brilliant university leader from Arequipa, the second most important city in Peru. The President's education was humanistic. He studied in Lima, where he received political indoctrination from Haya de la Torre. He did graduate work in Madrid and Paris.

The formation period of Alan García's Aprista "*promoción*" started in 1968, the last year of the first Belaunde administration, and lasted through the twelve years of the longest military dictatorship and the second Belaunde term in office, which ended in 1985. The earlier cadres had received, above all, a political preparation; starting in the 1960s the orientation was diversified. Sociologists, economists, managers, engineers, anthropologists, and other professionals are now among the new PAP cadres trained.

Since its inception, our movement has worked on the development of a plan of government. Since 1931, when our Immediate Action Plan was published, the PAP Central Committee has included a Secretary for this purpose. From 1980-1985 planning grew and consolidated under the expert guidance of Luis Alva Castro, then in charge of the National Commission of Government Planning (*Comisión Nacional de Plan de Gobierno, CONAPLAN*). He is now Second Vice President of the Republic, President of the Council of Ministers, Minister of Economy and Finance, and member of the Chamber of

Deputies. In addition, non-party professionals and specialists were attracted to work with *CONAPLAN*, and a planning team was created in each department of the country.

These years of work have created important assets for the government. The political responsibility for using these assets and conducting the affairs of the nation rests with a well organized team, led by the President, of men and women from all the Aprista classes. These range from the First Vice President and President of the Senate, Luis Alberto Sánchez, who is 86 years old, to Minister of Education Grover Pango and Minister of Agriculture Remigio Morales Bermúdez, who are 38 years old.

Our economic strategy has been focused on the most depressed areas in what is called the Andean Trapezoid. In these zones of misery, microregions have been created, which include several provinces and districts. The agrarian communities, whose roots go back millenia, have received the largest amounts of money ever. The countryside, in general, has been prioritized. President García frequently travels throughout the country to keep himself in direct contact with the peasants.

In the area of international finance, and in relation to the unpayable external debt, we have initiated a bold new policy. At the same time, we have stopped the deterioration of our currency, inflation has decreased notably, and interest rates have been radically reduced. The President has promulgated measures reducing red-tape and pressing the administration to serve the people, and not the other way around.

These are some of the positive measures applied in the last ten months. But we must also look at our continuing problems. The challenge confronted by the new Apristas in their democratic task is different from the obstacles that we confronted from the 1930s to the 1970s. At that time a feudal class reigned in the countryside. The agrarian reform knocked down the former masters of the land. What remains is an industrial, financial, and commercial plutocracy, which, due to its own shape, does not reach the extreme reactionaryism that characterized the powerful landlords (*latifundistas*), who used to live from the serfdom of the peasants. This plutocracy's view does not coincide with Aprismo, but it apparently recognizes the present democratic rhythm, and hopefully is "cured" of the *golpista* adventures which caused so much damage to all Peruvians.

Now other adversaries have sprung up from different camps: terrorism and drug trafficking. Hordes of youngsters have been organized against the acts of the new Apristas. They have been hypnotized by a Polpotian cult to commit insane destruction of life and goods, such as has never been seen in our country. Their scorn for human life is total. They destroy everything that means technical development. Their cruelest tactic is the use of children as explosives; they are usually destroyed by the bombs they carry without knowing what they are doing. For five years they have massacred humble peasants and artisans in small towns. Now, apparently checkmated in the countryside, they have turned to the city, where they are applying selective terrorism. This destructive ire must be stopped by the strong constructive action of our young managers in a double program of social and economic development in the depressed zones where terrorism is rooted.

Drug traffic acts in alliance with terrorism. It is the Peruvian modern plague. The centuries-old sowing and use of coca was never a problem. But when the big drug markets appeared in North America and Europe, the dollarized price of coca jumped to vast sums. No other crop comes close. At the same time that we must defend our own youth from drug-addiction, we are impelled to prevent cocaine from reaching the developed countries where there is a rich and avid clientele. We have suffered many assassinations of our young authorities who fight against the empire of the international drug-traffic bands in the lower parts of the jungle. Drug traffickers have suffered some defeats, but they are reborn due to the strength of money. Peru pays a stiff price to try to prevent drugs from reaching the powerful drug-consumer countries, who help us very little in this task. The price is not only part of our budget, but the lives of our young functionaries and police forces. We have been attacked by drug traffic and terrorism. The PAP must answer lawfully, rejecting the "an eye for an eye and a tooth for a tooth" response demanded by part of the citizenry.

Another challenge is our political competition with the "other" left, the United Left (*Izquierda Unida, IU*), which comprises an array of parties, including Marxist-Leninists. They struggle for the support of the same social sectors who make up our constituency. Some of the political forces of this less than cohesive conglomerate do not profess democracy, but use it only as a tactic. They have resorted to violent methods, to politicized strikes, to unrealistic petitions, and they are trying to make an endemic event of hunger strikes. The PAP, democratic by principle, must act within a framework of ample liberties to counter these forces, even though these adversaries aim for totalitarianism. This struggle may be solved in successive elections at different levels.

This is a general outline of the democratic challenge in Peru. We believe that the Aprista forces, overwhelmingly composed of young people, are strong. Public opinion polls reveal that President García is yet more popular now than when he won the elections. The Alan García administration, by its political and social actions, has created an increasing optimism in the population. We are resolute in our political and social plans to fulfill people's demands. We will defend ourselves democratically from our adversaries with the legislative strength derived from suffrage. We are working on the historical task of democratically transforming Peru for the benefit of the majority of the population.

The Democratic Response to Terrorism

JAVIER VALLE RIESTRA
Senator of the Republic
President of the Senate Commission on Human Rights (1985-1986)

The struggle for human rights in our hemisphere dates back to the days of the Spanish Conquest. For instance, there were the polemics between Fathers Vitoria and Sepúlveda on the issue of whether the American Indians had souls, resolved when Pope Paul I declared in the affirmative in a Papal Bull. There was also the apostolic struggle of Friar Bartolomé de las Casas in defense of the Indians; the conquest destroyed many things but it also did have some humanitarian aspects.

Terrorism is not a new phenomenon in the world. We had groups such as the Zealots, or the French terror of 1772, a sort of state terrorism, or the war to death of Bolívar against the Spanish royalist army. Let us recall the Russian terrorist-anarchists who assassinated Czar Alexander II. According to the revolutionary/military catechism, the objective is not only the elimination of private property, but also of the whole state. Their followers had one idea--the revolution--and only one goal--destruction. We have many other cases of assassinations: the Empress of Austria and the King of Serbia are two examples. In Spain, in 100 years, five prime ministers have been killed. But then what is the difference between that kind of anarchist terrorism and today's terrorism? The terrorism of those times was applied by only very small local circles. It was not known on a universal scale.

In Peru, terrorism is blown out of proportion and presented as a guerrilla threat to bring down the Peruvian state. The phenomenon of Shining Path terrorism in Peru has gone from a rural stage to an urban one, with violence now committed for publicity too.

What is the root cause of the Shining Path, a phenomenon which is not typical of Peru? As a book on terrorism and the late capitalistic crisis has observed, we should consider the idea of a late capitalism defined as a conflict-syndrome based on capitalistic processes of political integration and social marginalization. The author of that book is right when he asserted that as the consensus of the people increases on the legitimacy of the democratic system, so does the possibility that the most fanatical minorities may challenge such a system. We have seen this occur in Spain: as the process of giving autonomy to the Basque region took place, there was a sharp increase in the terrorist attacks by ETA. So an explanation of the terrorist phenomenon in Peru, which does not have an explanation in terms of popular appeal, may be found in the extraordinary popularity of Alan García, who on 14 April 1985 obtained almost 50% of the vote but today, in June 1986, probably has 75% support.

Is terrorism in Peru an issue of political crime or just of common crime? Political crimes are defined as based on idealistic hope to change society sometime in the future. Jurists consider two elements in appraising these crimes. One is the intentions of the transgressors and the second is the juridical injuries resulting from the acts. A political crime should have a state target. But we also have to look at the methods which are used. As was said in Nuremberg, cruelty of method makes terrorism lose its qualification as a political crime and makes it a common crime.

The Shining Path phenomenon corresponds very much to the definition of common crime. They use symbolic and communicative violence. They do not say anything explicitly but use cryptic messages. They do not have a government; they do not pretend to be recognized as legitimate combatants; they come together in space and they disband in time. And in this regard, they differentiate themselves from other guerrilla forces which have attempted to occupy certain territories, as was the case of the Cuban guerrillas in their time.

The statistics of the dynamite stolen in recent years are eloquent:

YEAR	STOLEN	RECOVERED
1980	4,420 kilos	67 kilos
1981	4,648	67
1982	1,645	524
1983	35,197	6,350
1984	105,208	51,617
1985	72,374	27,255
1986 (first months)	25,604	2,085

And consider the statistics to date of casualties in the struggle against terrorism: 2,534 terrorists; 2,432 civilians; 78 civilian authorities; 37 members of the armed forces; and 200 police members.

I am very much aware, as a former member of the Constituent Assembly, of the disparities we may find between the Constitution and the inequalities within Peruvian society. While the United States has a very vital Constitution which lets the people participate in the legacy of the founding fathers, and the Constitution is what the judges say it is, ours looks more like a semantic document. According to it, our parliament, a copy of European parliaments, has two chambers. I believe it would function better if it were unicameral. Furthermore, the Tribunal of Constitutional Guarantees, a sort of public ministry, has turned out to be an institution with a somewhat autocratic, perhaps fascist, vocation. Today, as before, the judiciary does not fulfill its tasks.

Vis à vis this situation we now have the leadership of Alan García giving hope to our people. The challenges are great. While 35 years ago Peru had 65% of its population in rural areas, today 65% of Peruvians live in urban areas. Infant mortality is 105 per 1,000 and life expectancy is 57 years, and we have areas in the country where it is only 47. The minimum wage is equivalent to US$30 a month. Within this framework, the Shining Path phenomenon looks more like a biological phenomenon than an ideological one.

The threat of terrorism has reached such proportions that it is stimulating somewhat autocratic tendencies within Peruvian society. Some sectors with autocratic tendencies are trying to put before us a very serious choice: state or democracy. And we find many who have praise for the Argentine model, although some Argentine generals now have been sentenced to long prison terms under the democracy. It is unfortunate that some Peruvian military and their disciples sustain, like the Argentine military, that for them, the friends of the terrorists and those who do not take a position against them are also terrorists.

The worst for them are the neutrals because from their midst terrorists recruit their rank and file. In Peru a former Minister of the Interior of the last Belaunde regime said that while the task was difficult, after 10 pm, anything that moved had to be shot. He maintained that of each 100 people killed in this fashion twenty might be members of Shining Path, and in the end the results for democracy would be positive. You know that in Colombia the magnificent figure of President Betancur was tainted by the events that took place at the Palace of Justice. I want to repeat what I said at that time to the Voice of America when I was in Washington: that authoritarian attitudes, instead of damaging terrorism, magnified it. In that unfortunate event more people were killed by the army than by the terrorists.

In Peru, under the current government and regardless of the serious warnings from President García, who said he would not fight death with death, the army tried to continue in what it had been doing since the previous administration. That is how we came to the situation in which the Senate of Peru had to investigate an act of genocide that took place in the high Andes of Peru. A non-commissioned officer and his troops landed in a helicopter and put all the women and children they encountered in one house, and in another one the elderly, then set the houses on fire and opened fire and threw grenades at the defenseless civilians.

As I was entrusted with the *in situ* investigation by the Senate, my investigating commission of senators conducted interviews at the headquarters of what we regarded as state terrorism initiated during the previous regime. When we questioned the lieutenant who was the responsible officer, he responded, as the records show, that a terrorist is not only one who takes up weapons, but also a three-year-old child who might be a potential terrorist. Furthermore, he had the nerve to assert that they were doing all this so that while the soldiers were resting on their machine guns we could, in our bourgeois style, become senators. My report was approved by the Senate, which has an APRA majority. The report stated that the act was a matter of common criminality and should not be judged under the military code. To have crimes punishable under the military code, you must have military acting under military conditions. According to the international covenants, the assassination of innocents is not a military act. You had the disgrace of the case of Lieutenant Calley, who committed similar acts in Vietnam. I think that punishment by itself is not enough. There must be some changes as well.

Why, after Nuremberg, have we state terrorism, crimes against human rights and against mankind in Argentina, Uruguay, and many other places? So far as we know there is no terrorist group that has achieved power and apparently they do not aspire to do so. The ETA has not achieved an independent state. The Red Brigades are now in retreat. Palestinians are far away from an independent state. But I have found that some people have a certain proclivity to play into the hands of terrorists.

Democracies have given away some things in trying to face the terrorist challenge. The Federal Republic of Germany, confronting the Bader-Meinhof gang, allowed arrests for more than 24 hours, limited certain rights, and restricted certain lawyers suspected of having terrorist connections. The West German government also allowed the storming of houses without warnings and roadblocks of the highways. But there have been no accusations whatsoever against the Federal Republic of Germany of having committed crimes of state terrorism in their struggle against the Bader-Meinhof gang. When the case was reviewed by the Tribunal of Human Rights in Strasbourg, it was said that Andreas Bader and Ulrike Meinhof had committed suicide while in prison. In the case of Italy, where we went from Utopia to reality, we have the case of a law which lasted for ten years stating that the police would not interrogate the terrorists. Now we are back to the practice of police interrogation previous to the interrogation by a competent judge. They have also applied the law of repentance, which favors those who repent, and in that way they decimated the Red Brigades after their capture of General Dozier, who was saved by somebody who gave up.

Spain, the country in which the Jesuit Father Juan de Mariana condoned tyrannicide, five prime ministers were killed in 100 years, and one million people were killed in the civil war, has not gone backward in its democratic profile. But in Peru there are a lot of people who would like to see us recommit to the fascists, and they call for the death penalty. We say no, not for this kind of phenomenon, we think it may be counter-productive. First, it is prohibited by the Constitution. We are also signatories of the Pact of San José, which forbids the restoration of the death penalty by those countries that have already abolished it. We would have to reform our Constitution and renounce the Pact of San José in order to adopt that legal aberration. Otherwise we would be putting ourselves outside the Inter-American system for the protection of human rights.

Second, it is well proved, as we have seen here in the United States, that rates of criminality do not go down because the death penalty is imposed. As Vanzetti said, we were just poor devils, now we are heroes. The death penalty does not have a discouraging effect; he who kills out of passion will do it with or without the death penalty. The terrorist willing to die as a result of an attack would be willing to face death as a result of public trial. With the camera crews, the TV, the presence of international organizations (Americas Watch, Amnesty International, the International League for Human Rights), the sentenced man or woman, with clenched fist raised and singing the Internationale, would happily die knowing that the death penalty has given him or her some mystique. After many years without open and public executions, Franco killed six people; it was only one year later that the ETA killed Prime Minister Luis Carrero Blanco in an act of terrorism. Yet in Peru today approximately 80% of the people are asking for the reimposition of the death penalty. It is only the democratic elites who are really holding out. The average person has difficulty understanding the psychology of the terrorist. I think that the motto of the terrorist could be the motto of the Spanish anarchist: I am not afraid of the consequences of my acts.

What can we do in the short term? We have taken some drastic measures, such as to rule certain provinces under a state of exception and curfew. That permitted us to approach some terrorist centers. But I repeat here what I have been saying in Lima. Putting the Army in charge of the situation is not the right formula. Because in a democracy such as that of Peru, with a popular leader such as Alan García, to be forced to govern with a curfew as in Haiti is really paradoxical.

The problem is two-fold. On one hand we have the terrorists; on the other hand, the guerrillas. Terrorism expresses itself in violence with a purpose of bringing the government to discredit and creating social panic. Guerrillas, in isolated operations, have assaulted military prisons. The police and the army can fight the guerrillas in the field, but we cannot fight terrorism with tanks in the streets.

Based mainly on the European experience, we have to develop an intelligence service. At the same time, it is necessary to take more juridical measures to impose severe sentences on the terrorists. Perhaps we need to introduce the principle of repentance (which some people consider unfair because it seems to condone the transgressions of those who have committed very serious crimes). Perhaps we may have to take steps that are foreseen in the Constitution when it says that a terrorist may be held for fifteen days, not just 24 hours. I also think a lot about the possibility of reforming the Constitution. We need, for instance, to have a more efficient parliament. Currently, in Peru, it takes about three years to get a bill through.

My purpose in speaking to you, who are part of the American

intelligentsia, is to ask you not to leave us alone. Peru is not El Salvador, which, despite its proximity to the United States, does not have Peru's historic experience. Peru is a place with a rich history. It is, to a certain extent, the Egypt of Indoamerica. The fall of Peru would be the fall of the Andes. And if, to prevent that fall, the state should turn fascist and autocratic, then the democrats would be facing a terrible dilemma: the violence of the terrorists or the terrorism of the state.

For my part, I think that there may be some hope and a better future if we can manage to retain the rights of *habeas corpus*, the parliament, and the constitution. We must do this with a socialist inspiration, because the countries that live, as we do, in the middle of these difficulties cannot really start a capitalistic process. That has not been fully realized by the masses. Between the reality and our theories we have new situations in Peru. In other words, within our democracy, we also have a revolutionary process. Confronted with the demographic pressure, urban and rural property have a rather high value. Peru has 1.2 million square kilometers and about twenty million people. We are over-populated, and that demographic pressure is destroying the institutions created by the Constitution. Our parliament has just enacted a bill which clears the way for the squatters to legalize their settlements. That is in recognition of a new world that is emerging, and I want this new world to remain within a democratic framework. What the insurrectionists would like to see is state terrorism in response to their own terrorism.

The man who has done the most against terrorism is Alan García. In a country with somewhat elderly structures, a thirty-six-year-old man is running the country. He is implementing our social democratic program with its anti-imperialist language, a language of unity needed in Latin America; with a denunciation of police corruption and the need for the immediate reorganization of the police force; an attack against the centers of drug traffic which were not touched by the previous government, although it knew quite well that they existed; and a denunciation of corruption in the state bureaucracy entrenched for centuries. To take care of the needs of the population, we must keep salaries above the level of inflation. (Traditionally salaries were kept below the level of inflation.) A Commission of Peace was created, which did not have much public support but tried to bring some kind of conciliation within Peru's borders.

On the other hand, as has been very clearly said by President García, the pyramid of distribution of wealth and income in Peru, in which 2% of the people are receiving most of the benefits, while the majority of the people suffer dire poverty, persists. In Peru we have two masses: one is made up of those who have work, who are organized in labor unions, who do form part of the establishment; and another one comprises those who are unemployed or underemployed, who have never had any knowledge of the historical and juridical system of Peru. Those masses are represented in the famous novels by Ciro Alegría and José María Arguedas. They comprise the person who, if asked about certain rules, attributes them to "General Peru." This is the Peru of Uchuraccay, the massacre of the newspapermen we investigated three years ago. As you know, in that village eight journalists were killed during the previous regime. We went there with journalists, the famous novelist Mario Vargas Llosa, and others to take a poll of the place. It is a trip that by land from Lima takes about two days and by helicopter takes only 45 minutes. This illustrates how we have in Peru the coexistence of different epochs, different historical times.

We are fortunate to have the teachings of Haya de la Torre and Alan García, a man with a historic consciousness. I do not want to play the role of a naïve apologist for him, but among Latin American leaders he is an outstanding statesman. He knows how to go about solving that problem of our unjust economic pyramid. If we can achieve a fairer distribution of wealth, we may have achieved a revolution without executions, gallows, or firing squads. This is the way I think we have to face the challenge of Shining Path. Of course it will take time to come through this process of social change and income distribution. Democratic socialism and Latin American integration, public morale, structural reforms of the constitution, and social and economic revolution are the ways to meet the challenge of terrorism in a democratic Peru.

Nationalism and Social Integration

GROVER PANGO VILDOSO
Minister of Education (1985-1987)
Deputy from Tacna

I come from a country that is living a democratic revolutionary process. Its characteristics are nationalism and the recognition that the people make history and should be the central concern of the governments.

I come from a country that has suffered historically not only from domination and dependency, but also from deep internal inequalities. These are manifested in the large population marginalized from the benefits that the 20th century provides to the industrialized countries of the Northern Hemisphere.

But in my country, led by a young President who is aware of the uniqueness of our experience, people are becoming conscious of the fact that the processes that have led to these inequalities are processes also endured by other countries of Latin America. My people perceive that the problems which exist today, precisely because they are problems common to the peoples of Latin America, are creating forces of integration which broaden the horizons of nationality, making them feel that our common past, scarcely disfigured by disagreements promoted from without, corresponds to our common future. This future is articulated both by our peoples and their rulers.

Let us consider some aspects of Peruvian and Latin American

reality. By whatever means a visitor arrives in Peru, the first observations will be of the coexistence of misery and wealth and of traditional and modern cultures. The visitor will be impressed with the racial plurality, the young age of the population, and the presence of noisy street vendors.

These contradictions are the symptoms of historical structural problems. We find, for example, that almost four out of the twenty million Peruvians are total or functional illiterates. Three million of them are women and more than a million and a half live in the Peruvian region known as the Andean Trapezoid.

Víctor Raúl Haya de la Torre, founder of the Aprista Party, used to say that every people experiences its daily life in its own space and time. That is, the relations the people establish with nature as a landscape, as a resource, as a challenge, and the relations the people establish in order to organize, to produce and to consume, constitute a historical configuration with an original rhythm, with its own sense of time and space, which makes that history parallel to the history of other contemporary peoples.

Many of the peasant communities of the Andean Trapezoid, which constitute the majority of the illiterate population, still live in their own space and time. This population not only has been historically marginalized by the state and the westernized and urban sector of the Peruvian society, but also by the illicit expansion of the haciendas. Because of this, they did not have access to agricultural technology or to the benefits of the state apparatus.

The coincidence on the map between poverty and illiteracy in Peru is such that I begin from this fact, which directly concerns the ministry for which I am responsible, in order to illustrate some of the challenges that our reality poses. It is the result of a problem of different space and time settings between the rural and the urban sectors, between the Andean Trapezoid and the coast and the jungle. We have a problem of simultaneous but not strictly parallel histories.

For this reason, the President of the Council of Ministers, Dr. Luis Alva Castro, said: "If nationalism does not stem from love and fraternity, from understanding and help for our poorest countrymen, then it is not nationalism. Nationalism is a moral sentiment more than a political banner, it is an imperative of justice more than a demand of the state, a solid and egalitarian basis of social conduct more than a claim for territorial boundaries."

This vision of nationalism can only be understood in its historical dimension, within the context of a country in which social sectors living in different space-time coexist. We must understand that it is not coincidental that there is no national project capable of uniting the efforts of all to establish institutions and processes which can produce and protect the development of democracy.

Our nationalism is rooted in our reality and recognizes the changes that occur through time and through human effort. We recognize that the organization of the manual and intellectual workers of the more modern sectors of the country has created political forces capable of making their presence felt in the government and of imposing options for emancipation from external domination.

In the last three decades, migration from the rural areas to the cities has changed the urban identity. The human settlements that have formed belts, especially around the coastal cities, have succeeded in expressing themselves politically and have developed strategies of resistance to marginalization. The conditions for a national project have begun to exist, with a capacity to gain popular support because people who were silenced have formed channels of expression.

There is a strong link between nationalism and social integration. We believe that the whole country loses when the structural defects and problem situations are not remedied. All of Peru loses when we have illiteracy, poor productivity, poor nutrition and health, neglected children, or deficient education. The delinquency in Lima and Cuzco, the explosive and insane political violence of terrorism, and the self-destructive violence of adolescent drug addiction offer lessons which we should not take too long to learn.

Peruvian society suffers from violence because it has incubated that violence in its history. As President Alan García said, in a forum in which strategies for developing the Andean Trapezoid were proposed, "To many Peruvians, to the members of the peasant communities, to their children who migrate and re-create communities in the squatters' belts around the coastal cities, Peru is a broad and alien world." One of the most important tasks that we, the new generations, have taken on is to return Peru to the Peruvians.

We know, with Jorge Basadre, historian of the Republican period, that our country is both sweet and cruel, full of problems but also of possibilities, and that it is threatened by two forms of lack of consciousness. These are that of the conservatives, who believe that nothing can or should change, and that of the incendiaries, who believe that true change will only be possible after the total destruction of all that is rotten and old.

We, the disciples of Haya de la Torre, have learned that the process will be gradual, and will go through the definition of social, economic, and regional priorities. Our social priority is to attend to the base of the pyramid: the poorest, the youngest. For them new jobs must be created, resources have to be made available, health and educational services have to be democratized.

Our economic priority is agriculture. We must produce what we consume and learn to consume only what we produce. We have to try to rediscover traditional and efficient technologies, to re-evaluate traditional native patterns of food consumption. There is an effort to make agricultural loans cheaper, and to democratize information in order to complement technologies.

Our regional priority is the Andean Trapezoid, where the democratic revolution should prove its efficiency and improve the quality of daily life. As Dr. Alan García has said, centralism, the parasitic dependence of Lima on the rest of Peru, must end. We have undertaken integration by means of deconcentration, debureaucratization, and micro-regionalization.

The intra-national process of integration is the response of a government of manual and intellectual workers, a political force born of the people. It is Peru's re-encounter with itself, the eruption of the Andes in the cities, the eruption of peasant organizations on the political scene, the new identity which defines its different shapes in music, in the informal economy, in the communal workshops and kitchens.

It is important to make clear that we do not perceive this social integration process or this nationalism as efforts at homogenization which would destroy regional and local identities. My country is multilingual and multicultural, and the new Peruvian generations know the difference between aspiring to unity and imposing uniformity.

We do not have to sacrifice, in the name of national unity, the infinite variety of the cultural values which, within their different space-times, have been created by our diverse communities as the splendid fruit of their spiritual creativity. Speaking in a country with the motto *e pluribus unum*, we emphasize with satisfaction our conviction that we will be a great country only if we learn to be united and we increase our capacity to communicate among ourselves by valuing the richness of our diversity.

I have talked about nationalism and social integration processes within my own country, but I would be blind and disloyal to concentrate only on our own problems and possibilities.

I must now talk in continental terms about integration of all peoples. I want to bring up some concepts expressed by Dr. Alan García Pérez a few weeks ago at ALADI (Latin American Integration Association) in Montevideo. The President recalled that for the political movement created by Haya de la Torre, integration has been held, since 1924, to be the secret for liberation. In those years the members of the movement followed José Enrique Rodó's call to act heroically in search of the truth. A young and intellectual movement was born, the University Reform, to reject obsolete methods, to reject the voice of authority at the university, which alienated us from our own reality.

The University Reform, as a fundamental movement in our America, was complemented by the echoes of the Mexican Revolution, anti-imperialist, profoundly agrarian. From these concepts and examples, Haya de la Torre later elaborated a philosophical thesis described by him as "Historical-Space-Time." He said that America was new for those late arrivals who conquered it, but for us it had an old reality in its own space and time. Haya de la Torre said that we were a "people-continent" and one historical entity. The rediscovery of this historical entity was the conceptual objective of a theory that he called Aprismo.

That young generation became aware that Latin America could not defend itself from underdevelopment without searching for its own identity, without speaking with one voice. Today we know that we have lost too much time, and it is necessary to recover the experience of that lost time. One hundred sixty years of our history teach us that there are no roads our countries can travel separately without meeting failure at the end. We must learn to walk united, not only because of the weight of theories or goodwill, but because of the demands of the crisis we are living through.

In face of today's most pressing problems, the most important being the external debt, there is no solution without integration. There is no possibility of development unless we do away with dependency, which is prolonged by the external debt and which results in death, unemployment, backwardness, and the consolidation, even within our societies, of the stronger over the weaker.

How can we articulate a tenable and dignified position on the external debt if throughout the continent centrifugal forces insist on the search for bilateral agreements, use financial intimidation and try to isolate those who demand changes? There is only one answer to these pressures: integration will allow us to affirm loudly and in chorus what it is difficult to say alone.

For this reason, we must recognize the contributions of the Sub-regional Andean Group, the Amazon Pact, SELA (Latin American Economic System), ALADI (Latin American Integration Association), and of the Cartagena Accord to the efforts of integration. We must also recognize the contributions of many forums, seminars, and regional workshops that have served to share and systematize experiences, to establish permanent channels of communication, and to make agreements which many times have paved the way for intergovernmental agreements.

To the extent that the shared problem of the external debt transcends the interest of those responsible for financial policy and affects all aspects of life in all our countries; to the extent that this problem leads us to perceive the substantive incompatibility between development and dependence, and also between solitude and emancipation; and to the extent that we are living through an historical hour, in which solidarity among us and dignity in the face of our creditors entail risks, we are obliged to exercise lucidity, as well as to make decisions in a spirit of bold and generous solidarity.

This is why we appreciate the very special meaning that the Contadora Group and the Support Group have for Latin America. Just as within a society every member must feel that he is regarded as a full person and must himself accord personhood to everyone else, so in international relations each nation must feel its own sovereignty and at the same time defend in solidarity the sovereignty of its sister nations. The commitment taken on by the Latin American peoples to build peace in Central America is a commitment based on sovereignty and solidarity. These two notions are also the axis around which it is possible to articulate a common position on the external debt problem.

We must clearly state, however, that political and economic integration alone are insufficient guarantees of a multidimensional and integral development. This is why we hail the growing consensus reached within the Organization of American States on the necessity of an integral and integrated development. The fact is that our countries, and especially their governing elites, have had the propensity to embrace one-dimensional development theories and projects. These have produced some benefits, but have also created frustration because our most pressing problems have not been solved. So the elites have re-discovered, in the daily life of the people, the point of reference for the effectiveness of any proposal for development. As Minister of Education of Peru and the person responsible for the direction of education, science and culture in my country, I have presented to the men and women of Peru an educational proposal which is synthesized in the phrase "Education for Life" and is based on the following principles.

To educate is to defend and to enrich the life of each human being, especially of those whose marginalization makes us question the meaning of our own lives. It is to defend, to strengthen, to enrich, and to direct toward the common good the potential of each Peruvian and of all Peruvians. To educate is to build justice and peace, with awareness of the right to uniqueness of each person, group, or historical collectivity. To educate is to fulfill fraternity as the highest form of peace and justice. It is the way in which people overcome the inexorability of competition and the struggle for survival. It is to construct national and Latin American unity.

To educate is to cultivate harmonious relations between man and nature, to know nature and to teach people to work with it in order to satisfy the needs of all. To educate is to preserve nature for future generations and to make national development possible. To educate is to recognize ourselves as a people with a rich, conflicted and painful past. It is to recognize ourselves as a people who can experience renewal by identifying a collective project which will free us of any dependency on imperialist powers and guarantee a different future, dignified and unified. It is to recognize ourselves as a people who reaffirm our commitment to freedom by exercising in daily life our choice of freedom and democracy.

This is the set of principles which underlie and nourish the prodigious cultural efforts in arts, literature, music. They have given Latin America a new and admirable presence in the world, a polyphonic voice which intones and sings a common hymn of hope. Understanding this, we want to announce that the one hundred years of solitude of the continent are coming to an end, and that a new and vigorous brother is being born to the peoples of the world.

We feel that we are part of the body of this collective new man and we have pledged our lives to his growth and strength, because as individuals and as a government, the fulfillment of the dream of Bolívar and of Haya de la Torre is the work that justifies us and transcends our existence.

The Parliament: Bulwark of the People's Power

LUIS ALVA CASTRO
Second Vice President of the Republic
President of the Council of Ministers (1985-1987)
President of the Chamber of Deputies (1987-1988)

In 1821, when our independence was proclaimed, our ancestors framed a hope and made a clear and courageous promise to establish democracy and to create unity in society through the parliament and based on a national consensus. The parliament is the origin of our political being, the home of our freedoms and the bulwark of our popular power.

It is for the fulfillment of this promise and for this hope that Peru has survived all this time. Workers, peasants, intellectuals, youngsters and old people, men and women: many have lived and died to keep this promise and this hope alive.

APRA is the inheritor of this promise. We are sure that in the immediate future the day will come on which the great republic--founded on freedom and on justice, stubbornly prepared to be sovereign and to build its own, marvelous destiny--will be a reality.

We are on an unknown path. We are trying to build a country with "Bread and Freedom" (*"Pan con Libertad"*) as was dreamed of by the creators of our movement. But we also attempt a new path under Alan García's renowned and hopeful leadership.

"The Parliament: Bulwark of The People's Power" is excerpted from the inaugural speech of the President of the Chamber of Deputies delivered at the Chamber on 28 July 1987.

In this task Peru cannot surrender. In the struggle that we are fighting today Peru's destiny is at stake. Fortunately we are not alone; our people and our legislators participate in the struggle. We, the legislators, want to be arm-in-arm and heart-to-heart in the first line of the vanguard. We want our nation to be a sovereign nation. We reject all interference. We condemn the imperialistic scheme to subjugate our fatherland. This struggle aims to build a democratic and sovereign nation, especially now that the whole world knows that Peru has arisen again, that its people are marching united, that Peru is struggling to find a courageous solution and that we have the moral right to be victorious.

On the verge of the beginning of the second millennium, Peru is trying to solve the huge crisis that could have led to a hecatomb. In this attempt and in its result, Peru will demonstrate that a nation conceived of and consecrated to liberty and justice will survive if it does not forget that on this huge battlefield, the first protagonist is the people. History has taught us, through Karl Marx, that the most important protagonists are not the individuals but the movements to which the people belong in order to achieve power.

Popular power has its place here in the Congress where, as Haya de la Torre said, the people meet to found the first power of the state, to return to the origin of their political being and to direct the Congress's organization with the utmost liberty. And it is in the Congress that, in each session, we maintain and reclaim the tradition and heritage of the initial movement which gave us our freedom. We must continue and improve this tradition and heritage of rationality, polemic and free concert of wills which bestows on the Parliament and the Republic their sense of security and permanence.

When there is stability in a country, security is not given too much importance because it is a parameter, something taken for granted, a quality in the lives of people. In our country the crisis is not an academic discussion but an everyday fact. This is why the concept of security is on the front page. We will only be able to find security in the stable and vigorous government of popular power.

Today's crisis is the result of the state's anachronistic and asymmetric structure. Because of this, almost all the institutions supporting the democratic and republican form of living have been on the point of collapsing. Midway between discouragement and desperation, between poverty and extinction, between hunger for bread and hunger for hope, our people have been on the verge of losing faith. Many of our fellow countrymen had already lost faith when in 1985 we arrived in government to inaugurate a new period of hopefulness for Peru.

The Parliament: Bulwark of the People's Power 59

This is why now, more than ever, faith is required. Fortitude, solid platforms and perspectives that reduce uncertainty are now proclaimed. Proposals that weaken doubt and institutions that recall the reasons they were created are now needed. We want a parliament that recalls the promises which its founders made, a parliament that knows that history will punish improvised actions, will not sanction torpidity and will reward coherency. We need members of the parliament who know that history will judge them not for their oratory but for their courage and efforts in creating a new Peru, a new society without exploited or exploiters.

We are at an important turning point. There are people who believe that the revolution will be made by killing peasants, sowing death among the most humble authorities and sowing terror in all sectors. This is not true! The truth is that life will rise above death.

Life and reason must be reaffirmed in Peru, and nobody should accept the game proposed by death's partisans. This is why the first thing this parliament has to do is to legitimize the deeds of the democratic institutions to end, through legal and revolutionary means, the problem of violence. When a society, through its parliament, renounces the death penalty, it has limited the power of its state over the life and death of its citizens. It cannot then consent that anybody, even for reasons of state, can continue to kill. We, the members of the parliament, will not allow it.

We cannot stop the killing of public servants by imitating the killers' questionable norms of conduct. We will have to use our moral strength, as the original power of the state, to eradicate torture and abusive police practices. To eradicate terrorism is not the same as to massacre terrorists. I want to declare with absolute firmness that the Chamber of Deputies, over which I have the high honor to preside, will never permit human rights violations, persecution of the innocent by accusing them of terrorism, or the use of torture as a method of investigation. We, the Apristas, have suffered in the past from these methods and can never permit this to happen to other compatriots.

I say these things as a proud member of this venerable congress and I reaffirm them as an old militant of a party that was born to make the social revolution and that will do so without ever abdicating its ideals, its brave tradition or the example of its martyrs who struggled, suffered and were jailed because of their faith in a great and just Peru. To follow this path means the parliament must recognize its origins in the thoughts of the founding fathers and at the same time to surpass them by making the state apparatus not a burden to the population, but the instrument of a free and democratic society. This is the only way to extirpate violence.

Let us recall the ideas of three Peruvians who, in our Republican period, have converted truth into history and history into a rebellious truth and have provided the underpinnings for our task.

One of them is Francisco de Paula González Vigil, who, in the dawn of the Republic, proclaimed, "We, the members of the Parliament, especially the representatives of our provinces, are the first power of the state and our resolutions are executed... the nation is looking at us at this moment and is waiting for our resolution in order to eternally cover us either with glory or with ignominy ...."

The second is that master of idealism, Víctor Raúl Haya de la Torre, who said that "The Peruvian Parliament has been able to enhance its quality and its prestige as the first power of the state and it has been able to inspire the Peruvian people with the security and hope that not everything has to be asked of the executive palace. Because there is another palace, more modest, but more authentic as an expression of the popular sovereign will...." Víctor Raúl added, "The parliament, as the expression of the popular will, must be a lesson, unknown for us during our hundred and more years of independent life, that must stimulate the hope that popular power can reach the superior stage of an organic democracy, which should not be other than a parliamentary democracy."

Much more present to us are the thoughts and words of a man who embodies, as no other chief executive, the multitudinous hopes of all Peruvians. He is a young and resolute president, who incarnates at the same time the best libertarian tradition and the sacred struggle for the most beautiful utopia. I speak of the Constitutional President of Peru, my *compañero* and my brother, Alan García Pérez. He had the courage to say: "Presidents can give signs of flexibility, but this in itself does not constitute democracy. What characterizes democracy is the existence of a solid, firm, and proud legislative power, independent of any outside influence. What characterizes democracy is the existence of this genuine representation in which the sentiment, the will, the dream, the past and the future of our people is expressed."

We who believe that social justice is not an oratorical discourse but a truth the world needs for survival have the obligation to speak in the language of the future. This means to reclaim the legacy of the founding fathers, but at the same time to build a different state. This we Apristas call economic democracy. The economic democracy that we will build "is the one that considers the human being not only as a member of a representative state which is governed by the will of citizens' majority, but also the one that considers the economic dimension fundamental among the rights and duties of that majority " (Víctor Raúl Haya de la Torre's speech of 20 August 1931).

Thus, our task is to create the basis for an Economic Congress (*Congreso Económico*) as an entity that should "contribute, with the technical support of all the participants, to the economic life of Peru: production, circulation, and consumption of the national and foreign wealth of the country.... With regard to national production, the Economic Congress will study its real productivity, its developmental possibilities, what our production is and what it could be, in harmony with the needs of the country...."

I am quoting the first APRA manifesto, whose ideological origin relates a political conception to its economic projection. These concepts are expressed in the *Manifesto to the Nation* (*Manifiesto a la Nación*), written in February 1932, when in the midst of persecution APRA clandestinely disseminated the truths and the lights of a project that today we are willing to teach and to convert into the most solid base for the reconstruction of this country as an authentic fatherland of unified workers.

But we are not going to limit ourselves to this. Our parliament, as a bulwark of the will of all Peruvians--the men of the sunny coast, those who live on the highest plateaus and those who inhabit the jungle--represents a nation with many faces, which in its history has accepted and responded to the challenge of its formidable geography. Our parliament must be the vanguard in the decentralization and integration process of the country.

This sovereign congress met once in Huancayo to give the nation a liberal constitution and met also in Chorrillos and in Arequipa during the ill-fated days of the war to keep alive the spirit of Peru as an independent nation. Our congress has been in session in different regions of the country when history has required it. Today, more than ever, the congress must be ready to obey the demand of the most diverse regions of the fatherland. That is why we will go out and meet where we are needed, where the people's voices will join with the voice of their representatives in order to revive the true democracy and in order to offer to the country the moral authority that this time of love and struggle requires and demands.

We are ready to work very hard to give the country fundamental laws. Some of them are long overdue. In addition to the law concerning the national Economic Congress, we must approve the proposed new laws creating the different regions, and the laws concerning the state's entrepreneurial sector, the Office of the General Comptroller, the Ministry of Foreign Relations, the new internal rules of the Chamber of Deputies, rent control, and the victims of terrorism.

Today I also want to make an important declaration. The Chamber of Deputies assumes through me the commitment to set in motion the committee to investigate the events in the penitentiaries[1]. The President has said we have nothing to hide. And we will hide nothing. If people are culpable the law will be applied to them. Where they are not culpable, we will stand up for those who risk their lives every day defending our democracy.

I also want to declare my decision to debate the amnesty law proposal, which is now in the Senate, as soon as it comes to the Chamber of Deputies.

It is our plan to create a highly specialized advisory system to be at the service of all the members of parliament, to equip it with a modern computer and word processing system which will be connected to the most important state data bases. We believe that in this way we will increase the efficiency of the congress and modernize the administrative and technical functioning of the two chambers as well as the work of the committees.

Thus, efficiency and supervision are the two objectives for our tenure. With regard to the latter, we will not only supervise the work of the parliamentary committees but will also establish a clear strategy to oversee the work of the executive. One aspect of this strategy will be to require the ministers to respond to a questionnaire prior to appearing in the Chamber. Only in this way will we be able to reach an equilibrium between the administrative work of the executive and the power to supervise of the congress.

Members of the Chamber: the future that we promised to the country has already begun. What yesterday was a visionary prophecy is now a promise of our time and a prerequisite for our common survival. The time of fulfillment has come. Bolívar's dream and Haya de la Torre's hopes presage a united, generous and renewed Latin America. Haya de la Torre admonished, "Either our fatherlands will be united in a great amphictyonic fraternity which makes Indoamerica the new home of real justice and integral freedom, or we will perish under the enslaving yoke of institutionalized barbarity" (Haya de la Torre, 7.28.41). Today the instruments for fulfilling the unification and integration objectives are in existence. The Andean Parliament

---

[1] On 18 June 1986 there was a coordinated revolt in three of Lima's penitentiaries. The revolt was violently ended by the armed forces. More than a year later, a Parliamentary Committee, led by Senator Rolando Ames, a member of the opposition, was elected to investigate the events.

and the Latin American Parliament must be strengthened for this region to fulfill its destiny. Bolívar today exists, struggles, and convokes, and it is only when his dream comes true that our America will be truly independent.

Perhaps it might be worthwhile to recall that next year, 1988, will be the fiftieth anniversary of the death of a great American: César Vallejo. His poetry signaled the rejection of artifical values. He is the emblem of liberation from foreign impositions, the symbol of reclamation of our Andean legacy and the creation of a just, beautiful, happy, and different fatherland in which free men are born and all the dreams and prophesies can come true. This is why I ask you to allow me to include a little poetry and art in this basically political message.

Next year will also be the 100th anniversary of the birth of the painter José Sabogal, the master who reclaimed the native heritage of the *indigenista* school in Peruvian painting.

In homage to Vallejo and Sabogal we must formulate a cultural policy which allows our old legacy be kept and at the same time makes real the new message of social change for our people. We are going to submit to the sovereign congress of the republic a proposal making 1988 the Year of Letters and Arts. The Year of César Vallejo and José Sabogal.

But we must go beyond this. Our efforts must be redoubled in our struggle to make Peru and Latin America return to themselves to search for their most original and genuine being. From these efforts will emerge a new fatherland and a new historical consciousness as were conceived of and designed by Sabogal, Vallejo, Haya de la Torre, and all our thinkers.

Finally, in this Congress, where our ancestors framed a hope and made a promise, I must pay the homage deserved to those who occupied the presidency of this Chamber before me in this present democratic period, my *compañeros* Luis Negreiros and Fernando León de Vivero. Thanks to their qualities as fighters for social causes, this house of freedoms and bulwark of popular power has not forgotten its origins and its reason to exist.

Members of the Chamber of Deputies of Peru: Today we are not representatives of a cornered and frightened state, or of a fatherland of people who have lost hope. We are the representatives of a people who are standing up and walking toward their destiny. A people who do not surrender. A people who venerate their awesome ancestry. A people who founded this house so we could represent them firmly and proudly. A people who have suffered much, who have struggled much, who have waited much, and who in the most dramatic hour of their history have chosen life.

For these reasons I would like to end this address with a phrase popularized by the President of all Peruvians, our *compañero* Alan García:

Compañeros, ¡viva la vida! (Long live life!)

Origin and Diffusion of The Shining Path in Peru

EUGENIO CHANG-RODRIGUEZ
Queens College of The City University of New York

It is generally recognized that the two most serious problems Peru is facing in the 1980s are the economic crisis and terrorism. The Shining Path, the main protagonist of terrorism, by far more active than the Tupac Amaru Revolutionary Movement (*Movimiento Revolucionario Tupac Amaru, MRTA*), is giving the concept of revolution a new meaning. This chapter summarizes the origins, development, ideology, and tactics of this perplexing Andean political phenomenon. It is based on eight months of research in Peru undertaken by its author before and after the seminar on "The Democratic Challenge in Peru" met at the Bildner Center.

By order of the Komintern, the Peruvian Communist Party (PCP) was founded in 1930 by Eudocio Ravines (1897-1970) and most of the six comrades who had helped José Carlos Mariátegui (1894-1930) to organize the Peruvian Socialist Party (PSP) in 1928[1]. The opponents of this PSP takeover and change-of-name established another socialist party or joined the Peruvian Aprista Party (PAP), founded in September 1930. The Peruvian Communist Party known as Shining Path (*Sendero Luminoso* or *PCP-SL*) is one of the splinter organizations of the original PCP. Some of the splinter parties of the PCP are no longer in existence. All of them, however, called themselves Peruvian Communist Party or Communist Party of Peru and chose to use the same initials: PCP (Chang-Rodríguez 1987:188-207, 375-78).

MYTHICAL ORIGIN

In the many efforts to explain the seemingly irrational violence in the Andean highlands, attempts have been made to relate it to themes developed in Inca myths created from the 16th century on. In order to lend rationality to historical developments otherwise difficult to explain, a preexisting religious and mythical framework has been used by Peruvian scholars, such as Oxford-trained Juan Ossio (1973) and Paris-educated Alberto Flores Galindo (1987), and sociologists, such as Jean-Marie Ansión (1987), a Belgian living in Peru since 1952. This conceptual framework, handled as a cultural device to reconcile the world as it is with the world as it ought to be, serves now to shed light on or decode the Shining Path political phenomenon.

According to this messianic interpretation, the PCP-SL is related to the ideology whose central theme is a unifying principle poised to reimpose an indigenous order on a world destroyed by the Spanish Conquest. In the 16th century, Guamán Poma de Ayala, an Indian chronicler, explained how the Andean world was turned upside-down by the arrival of the conquistadors. As, since time immemorial, people have coped with the extraordinary by myth-creation, the Andean Indians of colonial days, in order to satisfy their desire to reestablish the Inca order, created the myths of the *Taki Onkoy* and of *Incarrí*[2]. These and other theories posited that the colonial chaos could be dissipated by a superhuman agent sent to reorganize the Andean universe.[3] The mythical interpretation identifies *Sendero* with that messianic agent. The resurrection of the world of the indigenous people would be accomplished with the PCP-SL's four swords: the Marxist, the Leninist, the Maoist, and the sword of Comrade Gonzalo's guiding thought. Comrade Gonzalo and President Gonzalo are two *noms de guerre* of Abimael Guzmán (n. 1934), the founder and maximum leader of *Sendero Luminoso*. The prevailing revolutionary belief

---

[1] The PCP was founded in Lima on 20 May 1930.
[2] The first was an Indian resistance movement that started in Huamanga in 1565 and then spread to Lima and Cusco. Their leaders explained Pizarro's victory as a result of the defeat of the Indian divinities by the Christian god. As their gods had revived, they were leading the battle against the invaders in which female leaders and priestesses participated side by side with men. With time the Taki Onkoy became a symbiotic religious movement of pre-Columbian and Catholic beliefs in which political objectives were prominent. The Incarrí was Atahualpa, whose decapitated head would eventually rejoin his body. Cf. Arguedas 1956, 1967; Bourricaud 1959, Millones 1964, Ortiz 1970, and Ossio 1973:XXVIII.
[3] Cf. Maticorena 1981:441 and Macera 1984:27.

is that the new Andean response to the historical challenge should take a new form of revolution and not be simply a traditional rebellion.

Although *Sendero's* leaders are, in the majority, white and *mestizo*, the troops are mainly Indian and *mestizo*, just as they were in the struggle for political emancipation in the last century. It is then possible to conjecture that many of today's Andeans subscribe to President Gonzalo's preaching, which they identify with the myth of *Incarrí*. Nor is it inconceivable to imagine that in the present Andean storm the indigenous guerrilla fighters would view *Sendero* as the supernatural force capable of bringing about the symmetrical inversion of the existing chaos, not necessarily to return to a pre-Incan order, but to settle and put an end to disorder[4].

Although the PCP-SL has rejected the messianic thesis twice, its documents have called for a general uprising in the Andes and one of its high-ranking leaders has exalted the historical importance of Juan Santos Atahualpa (1710-1756) and Tupac Amaru (1741-1781) (Mercado 1982:53).

HISTORICAL ORIGIN

The origins of *Sendero Luminoso* can be traced to January 1964, when at the Fourth Conference of the PCP held in Lima there was a split of the supporters of the pro-Chinese faction from the main line of the PCP in order to establish another party with the same name, as was happening in other countries experiencing the repercussions of the Sino-Soviet ideological struggle. Jorge del Prado (n. 1910) was ratified as Secretary General of the faction faithful to the Soviet line (PCUSSR). The lawyer Saturnino Paredes Macedo, on the other hand, was elected Secretary General of the break-away faction, thanks in part to the assistance rendered by Abimael Guzmán, then a philosophy professor at San Cristóbal de Huamanga University and leader of the PCP committee in Ayacucho[5]. The Red Flag (*Bandera Roja*), the official journal of the new PCP, served to distinguish it from Jorge del Prado's faction, the PCP-U, which published the weekly *Unidad*[6]. The splinter group, the PCP-BR, postulated the study of Mariátegui

---

[4] After all, for the Andean man, the notion of returning to Inca order is nothing more than a metaphor conjured up to indicate the establishment of a new order (Ossio 1973).

[5] Ayacucho is the name of a Peruvian department and of its capital. It means "corner of the dead" in Quechua. Peru, a centrally governed republic, is, like France, politically divided into departments. Each department is divided into provinces.

[6] A useful book about what happened in that historic PCP meeting is PCP, Comisión Política, Acerca de la historia del Partido Comunista Peruano y de su lucha interna, n. p.: Ediciones Bandera Roja, 1968, 90 pp.

and the launching of armed struggle. It firmly believed that revolutionaries must not await the spontaneous development of subjective conditions for revolution; on the contrary, it advanced the idea that true revolutionaries ought to create, develop, and organize the conditions (Mercado 1986:17). The V National Conference of the PCP-BR, held in November 1965, adopted Mariátegui's characterization of Peruvian society as "semifeudal" and "semicolonial," and followed Mao Zedong when it adopted as a revolutionary tactic the protracted people's war that spreads from the countryside to the city. Accordingly, it was agreed to adopt Chinese strategy and tactics in an extended popular war, organize guerrilla fighters, and establish bases of support. The Revolutionary Armed Forces they envisioned called for an alliance of peasants and urban workers, with the former in the first line of command.

The Movement of Revolutionary Left (MIR) guerrilla warfare led by the APRA rebel Luis de la Puente Uceda and Guillermo Lobatón carried out a series of attacks in the Andes and the jungles of Central Peru in 1965. President Fernando Belaunde[7], in the second and third years of his first administration (1963-68), assisted by the United States, fought the insurgency. With the death of the two leaders and the capture of many in the guerrilla ranks, the subversive outbreaks were quickly suppressed and by the beginning of 1966 completely snuffed out. However, the historical revolutionary experience, inspired by the focal theory, demonstrated that the Quechua-speaking peasants could still join forces with the whites and *mestizos* in a union of conspiracy.

The MIR guerrilla experience generated more internal problems for PCP-BR. During this time, Abimael Guzmán, in charge of *Bandera Roja* editorials, tried to distance himself from the inner fights in the party leadership until he presided over the Second Plenary Session of the PCP-BR Central Committee in February 1970. The PCP-BR then split into two camps: one controlled by Paredes; the other by Abimael. The Paredes faction kept the control of the organization linked with the Chinese Communist Party (PCCH). Guzmán's faction retained *Bandera Roja* and entrenched itself in the universities. One of its most active organizations was the Revolutionary Student Front (*Frente Estudiantil Revolucionario, FER*), which used a letterhead with

---

[7] Traditionally the surname Belaúnde has been spelled in Spanish with an accent mark on the letter u. Architect Fernando Belaunde Terry, however, never used the graphic accent mark.

the slogan: "*Por el Sendero Luminoso de Mariátegui*" ("Through Mariátegui's Shining Path"), from which the unofficial name and abbreviation given to them by the press and government are derived. One of the most important FER cells was active at the University of Huamanga (founded in 1677 and reopened in 1959 after eight years of inactivity), where Guzmán had been teaching since 1962. He had been hired by Efraín Morote, then president of the university, and believed to be one of *Sendero's* theoreticians (Pedriali 1984:1).

FIRST PERIOD (1970-1980)

Periodization of *Sendero's* history could be made along organizational and developmental lines. A tentative chronological division of its history that takes into account its first decade of organization during the military regime and its armed actions during the two subsequent constitutional administrations seems to be more practical, as it gives us three clearly defined periods. When more facts are known about this clandestine organization and more documents are available a sounder periodization will emerge. Raúl González (1983), Cynthia McClintock (1983), Lewis Taylor (1983), David Scott Palmer (1984), Carlos Iván Degregori (1986), Henri Favre (1987), Manuel Jesús Granados (1987), and other researchers on the subject have faced this problem.

From the moment that the PCP-SL was established, its most distinguished and undisputed leader has been Abimael Guzmán. At the beginning his main concern was to present *Sendero* as a strong organized party at the national level working principally out of the University of Huamanga. Although he lost no time in calling for armed struggle, he set himself immediately to learning Mariátegui's teachings and readapting them for the purpose of rebuilding the party along organizational and ideological lines to serve as an apparatus for the advancement of the people's war. In 1967 the PCP-BR Central Committee had explained that "Mariátegui's path" meant "in theory to adhere to Marxism-Leninism; in practice, to develop revolutionary violence to smash reactionary violence and so to implant the dictatorship of the proletariat" (Mariátegui 1967:II).

In 1970 the PCP-SL was already convinced that Mariátegui's most substantive contribution was his ability to infuse Marxism with philosophical irrationality by reconciling Marx with Proudhon, by uniting Marxism with anarchist ideas, and by transforming himself, as had Georges Sorel (1847-1922), not into a revisionist of the author of *Das Kapital*, but into a revitalizer and continuator of his works. The Peruvian thinker, as did Mao, showed them that the Bolshevik experience generated its own contradictions and that it behooved third world revolutionaries to act in their own way, according to their reality and psychology, and, above all, taking into consideration their historical tradition. The *Sendero* leaders embraced Mariátegui's explanation of the final struggle and his theory of the revolutionary myth. He revealed to them that the Bolshevik Revolution, according to Marxist dialectics, brings in its entrails the seeds of its own replacement with a better revolutionary ideology and praxis. His articles on feminism helped *Sendero* strategists to develop the widespread tactical use of women in armed actions.

From 1970 to 1975 the PCP-SL channelled its activities though several subsidiary labor and student organizations. While they cherished and reread Mariátegui's most radical writings, they also learned from Mao's works, particularly his book on new democracy and his volume on guerrilla warfare. In October 1975 the PCP-SL summarized its evaluation of Mariátegui, justified its leadership and revolutionary mystique, and concluded that for a revolutionary, prison is but an occupational hazard (PCP 1975:24-25).

After spending several years in "readapting Mariátegui," the PCP-SL undertook the hard job of "reconstructing the Party" to adapt it to the requirements of the final struggle. To achieve this objective, they sent their cadres to the Ayacucho rural zones in order to convert the peasants and train them in revolutionary violence. Because of the high percentage of illiteracy (75% of the adult population, according to the 1961 Census), *Sendero* opted for oral communication and left the written expression for the upper and middle echelons of the Party. This decision might explain why the PCP-SL has published very few documents.

Yet when proselytizing, *Sendero* placed most of its emphasis on teachers, university students, and the lower economic classes. During this time it strongly supported labor claims and strikes by the powerful Union of Peruvian Teachers (*Sindicato Unico de Trabajadores de la Educación Peruana, SUTEP*). Support was given directly or indirectly, through organizations *Sendero* infiltrated, such as the Front of the Teaching Class (*Frente Clasista Magisterial*) (Reynoso 1979:145-53).

From the very beginning, *Sendero's* policy was based on rejection of any kind of legal order, above all when it applied to organization, propaganda, and action fronts, in all of which it acted clandestinely, following Maoist experience closely. Its praxis was founded on four premises: 1) that Peru is both semifeudal and semicolonial; 2) the bourgeoisie is bureaucratic; 3) that the revolutionary war is to proceed from the countryside to the city; and 4) that the country is living in a revolutionary situation. The principal focus of operation was at the University of Huamanga. There the *Senderistas* were in control of the Executive Council, the Student Federation, and the Union of University Professors. No wonder Abimael Guzmán was able to recruit some fifty professors and students, such as Luis Kawata, the brothers and sister Osmán, Ostán, Raúl, and Katia Morote Barrionuevo, Julio Casanova, and other future important leaders of his movement. Their program centered on the defense of the university because it was the heart of cultural life in Ayacucho; it also generated income from different sources.

Activities in other universities of the country were likewise significant. As they were carried out in the main through FER and the Federation of Peruvian Students (FEP), in a a few years *Sendero* militants gained control of the student unions of the universities of Tacna and Huánuco and made their presence known in most universities of metropolitan Lima. In the political sphere, *Sendero* communiqués and flyers mainly attacked revisionist communism and its pro-Soviet followers in Peru, the *PCP-Patria Roja*, the *MIR*, and *Vanguardia Revolucionaria*. In 1974 Guzmán's followers lost control of the Student Federation and the Executive Council of the University of Huamanga. Some professors who had been sympathizers began to withdraw from the scene. The last time *Sendero* members participated in teachers' congresses was in 1975, when they presented a thesis in defense of the university. From that time they abstained from open debates and public participation in order to dedicate themselves to underground work. *Sendero* kept off the streets and did not participate openly in public meetings, strikes or parades. The loss of influence at the University of Huamanga was compensated for by the proselytization of the peasants, the urban and rural lower classes, the Indian communes, and the workers of the small Ayacucho villages. They put special emphasis on their schools for the indoctrination of adolescents. Most of their political activity, however, remained hermetically closed to the general public. They organized their cadres with extreme precaution.

The change of leadership in the People's Republic of China (1971) and President Richard M. Nixon's visit to Mao (1972) and the consequent Sino-American rapprochement had repercussions in the Andes. *Sendero* came out to defend Mao Zedong while censuring the new Beijing government. *Sendero* militants emerged from underground work to express outwardly their preferences and rejections and to intensify their non-university activities with the purpose of strengthening its links with the different unions. Because, in their view, in a revolutionary situation the struggle to reform no longer mattered, since it only dulled the true revolution, *Sendero* opposed the national strike of July 1977 and preached abstention in the election of the representatives to the 1978 Constituent Assembly. When election time drew near, young *Senderistas* ran through the streets, cheering revolution, counselling abstention from voting, and painting the walls with slogans such as "Down with the Bourgeois State!" and "Long Live the Armed Struggle!"

In April 1978 the PCP-SL pamphlet, ¡*Contra las ilusiones constitucionales y por el Estado de la Nueva Democracia*! (*Against Constitutional Illusions and for the State of New Democracy*!), justified revolutionary violence, history's midwife. The following September the PCP-SL published ¡*Desarrollemos la creciente protesta popular*! (*Let Us Encourage the Growing Popular Protest*!), another important document (Rojas 1985:332-33).

On 17 March 1980, during the Sixth National Congress of the PCP-SL, the Central Committee in its plenary session declared that the Party had been reconstructed and that the pre-war period had ended (Gorriti 1984:18). When *MIR* and *Vanguardia Político-Militar* contingents joined *Sendero*, the Party leadership felt that it had the minimum number of troops required to set the popular war in motion. The situation improved when later in 1980, a break-away faction of *Vanguardia Revolucionaria-Proletaria* and a detachment from the *PCP-Patria Roja* known as *Puka Llacta* (Red Land, *Tierra Roja*) joined forces with them. The new adherents adapted to *Sendero's* vertical organization (R. González 1982:66-68).

SECOND PERIOD (1980-1985)

With the restructuring of the PCP-SL, and the adaptation of its ideology to create a machine for action, *Sendero* was ready to start the armed struggle in motion early in 1980. Drawing from the mistakes made in the past in Peru and the successful people's war in China, *Sendero* strategists approved three steps: 1) agitation and propaganda by perpetrating acts of sabotage to make the people aware that a popular war was beginning; 2) an offensive against the state and its military forces through direct confrontation in order to first acquire armaments and later establish liberated zones to be used to initiate the final phase; 3) an all-out war in which the country would dominate the city (R. González 1982:67). The first phase of the armed struggle was approved at a PCP-SL Plenary Assembly on 17 March 1980 (Gorriti 1984:18). There it was made public that the high command military plans and war strategy had already been chosen. Four days later, in a remote community in the Department of Ayacucho, Abimael is purported to have said in his commencement address to the graduates of the first military school:

> The time of defenseless hands, empty of weapons, is over. Today we begin to speak with fire: Let the masses rise up, let the peasants rise up under the banner of Marxism-Leninism and Mao Zedong's doctrine. We bring the past to an end and open up the future. The key is action; the objective, power! (Mercado 1988:27)

Two months later, on 17 May 1980 (PCP 1986:3,16)[8], the eve of the Peruvian general elections, *Sendero* began the armed struggle. In the small Ayacucho village of Chuschi, 45 miles southwest of Huamanga, several hooded *Senderistas* burned ballots boxes and election materials. Two days later, the policeman protecting the Nicaraguan Embassy in Lima was attacked by a group of hooded men who snatched away his machine gun. More armed actions followed, such as the attack on the Embassy of the People's Republic of China, in front of which *Sendero* hung a dead dog, "Inca symbol of contempt and attack" (The Committee to Support the Revolution in Peru 1985:6). According to an official count, *Sendero* perpetrated 219 terrorist acts in 1980 (Flores Galindo 1987:324).

At the end of 1980, the PCP-SL Central Committee held their Tenth Plenary Session and reviewed the actions they had taken. They evaluated and approved them and ordered that the offensive be generalized to comply with their current military phase. The purpose was to sharpen class differences in order to provoke military intervention. They were acting as though heeding the advice given by Manuel González Prada (1844-1918), ideological precursor of Mariátegui: use violence to gain justice because true liberty is born bathed in blood (González Prada 1940:164). Perhaps they remembered that Marx had observed that in revolutionary matters, the more pain experienced, the better the child brought into the world, and most likely they also remembered that González Prada had said that "Peru is today a plain dried by the sun; a spark, a single spark will ignite the entire nation:

---

[8] Several newspapermen and even some sympathizers give 18 May 1980 as the date of the begining of Sendero's armed struggle, as does Rogger Mercado (1987:21). An official Sendero document is very clear on this matter: "17 May 1980, not May 18, as the reactionaries say in order to confuse that date with the day of their elections, and others repeat" (PCP 1986:28).

the first to be destroyed will be the leaden soldiers" (González Prada 1941:232). Although first published in 1941, this image was written many years earlier than Mao's metaphor of the spark that sets the countryside ablaze.

Shortly after the first police station was attacked in Tambo on 11 October 1981, the Government declared a "State of Emergency" in five provinces of the department of Ayacucho. In the next few months other police stations were attacked. The most daring of the *Sendero* exploits was on 2 March 1982 at 11:30p.m., when five hundred *Senderistas* occupied the city of Ayacucho. They assaulted the Headquarters of the Civil Guard, the building of the Peruvian Investigative Police (PIP), the Headquarters of the Republican Guard[9], and took over the main prison, where they sang their revolutionary songs, raised the red flag, and liberated 304 prisoners (297 men and 7 women), among them, the celebrated guerrilla fighter Edith Lagos. After availing themselves of an ample supply of arms, they abandoned the city.

After this temporary and sensational occupation of the departmental capital, with a population of 80,000 people, the guerrilla offensive was stepped up. High tension towers were dynamited, bridges destroyed, and police stations, barracks, banks, and business establishments were attacked. Many actions were conducted against the courts, labor recruitment headquarters, government, tax, and voter registration offices, city halls, and ministries. The *Senderistas* even launched attacks against several of the offices of *Acción Popular* (AP), the ruling party. During this initial military phase, the *Sendero* vanguard briefly occupied small villages. Often they meted out punishment to policemen, soldiers, and civil authorities whom they accused of war crimes. Their personnel were armed with equipment captured from the police and armed forces and from haciendas and mines: machine guns, light firearms, and explosives. They also provided themselves with homemade arms. When food and medicines were needed, they confiscated them from stores and pharmacies owned by opponents to their cause. To broaden the scope of their authority, they increased the precision and daring of their lightning attacks on military targets.

Soon the armed campaign of the *Senderistas* confused those who believed that the tactical timetable of their guerrilla fighters dictated that they concentrate only on rural objectives and that the last phase

---

[9] The Peruvian Police Force is formed by the Civil Guard, the Republican Guard and the PIP (Policía de Investigaciones del Perú). They do not form part of the Peruvian Armed Forces, which comprises the Army, the Navy and the Air Force.

would involve a march on the cities. They did not realize that *Sendero's* plans also included propaganda for the armed struggle via action, which they call "propaganda and armed agitation" (PCP 1986:34-35). Spectacular exploits are preferred to press conferences. For them, better than newspaper, radio, and television publicity are hanging dogs on lamp posts, blackouts, and armed attacks on embassies. These actions might have been staged as an attention-getting mechanism to demonstrate the military and organizational prowess of the legions involved in the initial phase of the armed struggle. Blowing up electrical transmission towers, capturing arms and dynamite, and other bellicose actions might have been at times strategic training exercises to test the soldier in his or her first experience under fire and also to judge the patience of the government and its resistance and reaction capacity. The *Senderistas* extended themselves in every way in the Indian communities and small towns to make contacts and gain sympathy. When conditions warranted it, they recruited people. They shared provisions and punished anti-social elements, such as usurers, thieves, cattle rustlers, and abusive people. They lectured both in Spanish and Quechua to explain the reasons for the generalized misery as well as their belief in the inevitability of the triumph of the people's cause, and the creation of a new and more just society. In short, they promised to restore order to the Andean world. This path of hope they painted received accolades from well-meaning supporters.

During this period, *Sendero* enjoyed the advantage of surprise attacks on the police, who were forced into a defensive posture, unable to recover quickly because of it. The main theatre of operations was still Ayacucho, the most depressed region of the country after Puno. Apart from political considerations, one might well ask if there were other factors which contributed to the relative success of their first years of activities. The police analyzed the *Senderista modus operandi* and reached the following conclusions: 1) surprise tactics are employed in the mobilization of the squadrons; the attack is made and immediately thereafter the militants conceal themselves in some community or other, or they return to their daily occupations, and 2) excellent use of geography (R. González 1982:46); they move, in accordance with Mao's doctrine, like fish in water. Many *Sendero* activists were very young, barely in their teens[10]. Their elders seldom

---

[10] This policy of coopting very young people is explained further on. Among the many teenagers arrested and charged with Sendero terrorist acts is Gregorio Mitma Tineo, who coldly confessed in 1988 in front of the TV cameras and newspaper reporters to having assassinated three executives of the Agrarian Bank and having participated in the killing of Reverend Víctor Acuña and two policemen. He and one of his teenage accomplices were the

joined their fighting ranks, but they backed their militant sons and daughters. The support of the villagers and the lack of sufficient police reinforcements contributed to their success.

On 18 August 1982, at a meeting with the Association of Foreign Press Correspondents, Luis Pércovich, Minister of the Interior, identified five ideologues and eleven top leaders of *Sendero Luminoso*. The ideologues were Abimael Guzmán, Luis Kawata, Osmán Morote, Hildebrando Pérez Huaranca, and Antonio Díaz Martínez[11]; the top leaders were Abimael Guzmán, Elizabeth Cárdenas ("Betty"), Julio Casanova, Carlota Tello, Ondina González, Juan Carlos Florián, Nelly Cárdenas, José Kullich, Víctor Quintanilla, Augusto de la Torre Guzmán, and Julio César Mezzich (R. González 1983:35). The guerrilla Edith Lagos, a nineteen-year-old former student of the University of San Martín de Porras, was found dead on 3 September 1982. Her funeral in Huamanga was attended by some 15,000 people, almost one fifth of the city's population. Afterward guerrilla activities and acts of terrorism multiplied.

On 26 December 1982 the Belaunde government responded by placing nine adjacent provinces of the Departments of Ayacucho, Apurímac, and Huancavelica under military control. The intervention of the armed forces in the war zone accelerated the police counterattack against *Sendero*, particularly by the *Sinchis*, a special detachment of the Civil Guard trained in counter-insurgency operations by the American Green Berets during the guerrilla period of the mid-1960s. All this resulted in an increase in the number of casualties on both sides and amongst uncommitted civilians. At this juncture, *Sendero* carried out successful raids and failures, and confronted friendly and unfriendly Indian communities. It was forced to take two, three, and four steps back for each step forward. This meant that *Sendero's* situation began to get worse. While the stage had been set in motion with soldiers from the so-called people's army "forged in the struggle," successes were no longer as impressive. Nevertheless the order to continue pressing against the government remained. They continued their actions against the state through direct confrontation with the police and armed forces to guarantee supplies of war materials. This strategy paid off because a few months later the PCP-SL initiated its political strategy of "conquering bases," that is establishing, maintaining, and

---

two detainees accused of participating in the murder of Admiral Jorge Ponce Canessa (Puertas 1988:36).

[11] Díaz Martínez was killed during the Armed Forces attack on the rioting Lima prisons on 18 June 1986.

developing bases of support for the expansion of the bellicose campaign leading toward their future "great leap forward" (PCP 1986:4-5).

One of the most-discussed events in the Peruvian press in 1983 took place on January 21, when seven *Senderistas* were killed by the people of Huaychay, a very impoverished community high in the north of Ayacucho some 12,000 feet in altitude. This then-rare act against the Andean guerrillas prompted the visit of seven reporters to the scene. Lima papers had sent them to investigate whether the police or the military had anything to do with the massacre. These men, plus a Quechua-speaking colleague from a newspaper in Ayacucho, were assassinated on 26 January 1983 in Uchuraccay, some seven miles to the south of the community where the guerrillas had been killed purportedly under the direction of the *Sinchis*. Faced with public indignation, President Belaunde named an Investigating Commission, whose most prominent member was Mario Vargas Llosa[12].

On 22 February 1983 the Lima papers reported that official sources in Ayacucho had confirmed the death of Carlota Tello Cutti, "Comrade Carla." She and Edith Lagos, whose life also ended in the same region, are considered to have been the most effective and mobile female military commanders of *Sendero*. The armed conflict continued; San Cristóbal Hill in Lima was lit by torches forming the hammer and the sickle, repeating what *Sendero* had done in Huancayo and other cities.

A new picture began to emerge. The intensification of the war with its growing number of participants in military action and a greater number of people directly affected by these actions generated outbursts of opposition in different places. A great deal of resentment was caused by the threats and punishments dispensed by the guerrillas themselves to those who got out of line. Furthermore, the peasants began to resent *Senderista* interference and control of farm production because they did not like to be ordered to produce only for their immediate personal needs and they did not understand *Sendero's* policy of depriving the city of needed food. These tactics and other austerity policies led people to rebel in some Indian communities. In addition, many community markets were closed down by *Sendero*, forcing

---

[12] Abraham Guzmán Figueroa and Mario Castro Arenas were the other two members of the Commission. After investigating in situ, interviewing authorities and witnesses, reading their advisers' reports, and ignoring the press charges that the Commission in reality was interfering with the administration of justice, the three drafted their report to the President of the Republic.

peasants to travel even longer distances and spend more of their hard earned money to buy salt, matches, candles, and other basic goods. The so-called "executions of traitors to the movement, informers, and police collaborators" were condemned by many sympathizers both in the city and in the countryside.

The PCP-SL kept up the military pressure on other Andean and coastal areas. The mayor of Cerro de Pasco was murdered on 8 November 1983. The new *Sendero* offensive, waged in several districts, obliged the government to expand the Emergency Zone first to eleven provinces and then in 1984 to 13 out of the 140 provinces of the country. The entire zone was subject to the general control of the military commander based in the army barracks located in Ayacucho. The accusation that a dirty war was being waged in the Emergency Zone became more prominent in the press and television, with charges being supported by interviews of relatives of the persons arrested who then disappeared. The terrible phenomenon of the "disappeared" people (*desaparecidos*) and human rights violations in Peru received more and more national and international attention, especially after each discovery of a clandestine cemetery of tortured and executed peasants.

Other AP mayors were assassinated. On 8 July 1984 *The New York Times* reported eight policemen killed by *Senderistas* on the previous day, bringing the total number of victims to 250 in two weeks; these included 27 peasants in the town of Chicuas, 62 miles from Ayacucho. All this provided the government with a reason for the two-month extension of the state of emergency on July 6 (*The New York Times* 8-8-1984:L5). The mayor of Huancayo was killed on 24 July 1983. The state of emergency had not deterred the terrorists.

On 22 February 1985, a few days before Pope John Paul II visited Peru, Amnesty International circulated a document on the violations of human rights in Peru. The Belaunde administration did not pay any attention to the Amnesty International report, just as it had ignored the correspondence and other communications sent by that body. At any rate, the violence escalated. More and more policemen, military personnel, and civilian authorities fell victim to the terror. Thousands of persons were detained.

When the 1985 general elections approached, the PCP-SL promoted abstentionism, circulated threatening flyers, and even mutilated the fingers of some peasants from Ayacucho, Huancavelica, and Pasco because they had declared their intention of participating in elections[13]. In February of that year, its Central Committee issued the document *Don't Vote! Instead, Expand the Guerrilla War to Seize Power for the People!* (*¡No votar! ¡Generalizar la guerra de guerrillas para conquistar el poder!*) There they justified their actions and stressed the following: 1) the United Left is "the most blatant expression of the road of electoral opportunism and parliamentary cretinism in the country;" 2) "power can only be seized through revolutionary violence," which in Peru means "armed struggle from the countryside to the city;" 3) the PCP-SL has multiplied its membership and gained prestige inside and outside the country; and 4) it has built a People's Guerrilla Army of thousands of combatants and hundreds of People's Committees[14].

Notwithstanding this exaggerated appraisal, the general elections took place without incident on 14 April 1985. Ten days later, however, three men, armed with machine guns and explosives, seriously wounded Domingo García Rada, president of the National Electoral Board. While people anxiously awaited the voting results, three terrorists shot at close range Luis Aguilar Cajahuamán, who had just been proclaimed APRA Deputy. Other mayors and leaders of the PAP were murdered in cold blood. This was the way *Sendero* responded to the official recognition of the PAP victory with 53% of the votes, which gave the PAP the presidency of the republic and majorities in the Chamber of Deputies and in the Senate[15].

THIRD PERIOD (1985-   )

This period of the PCP-SL began the day Alan García assumed power on 28 July 1985. In his address to the nation, the 36-year-old

---

[13] Peruvian voting procedure includes the dipping of the voter's index finger in a hard-to-remove dye to avoid repeated voting.

[14] The entire document was unofficially translated by Sendero admirers in California and published immediately after another document in a booklet with a red cover. Cf. Central Committee of the Communist Party of Peru, Develop Guerrilla Warfare. Don't Vote! Instead, Expand the Guerrilla War to Seize Power for the People! (Berkeley, California: The Committee to Support the Revolution in Peru, 1985), pp. 25-35. Cf. with the Spanish version reproduced in Colombia. "¡No votar, generalizar la guerra de guerrillas para conquistar el poder para el pueblo!" in Un Mundo que Ganar, London, No 3 (1985):52-59. This quarterly magazine, printed in Bogotá, Colombia, is published and distributed by A World to Win, a quarterly journal published in London.

[15] The first official results of the elections gave García 45.74% of the "valid" votes, which included the void and blank votes, by decision of the National Electoral Board, and thus required, according to the 1979 Constitution, a second election between the two candidates with the highest number of votes. As the official percentage was challenged, Alfonso Barrantes, United Left candidate, who obtained 21.25%, the second highest percentage, declined to participate in the second round. Subsequently, García was proclaimed President for having received 53.10% of the valid votes, excluding the void and blank votes.

President outlined his government's plans and promised to be implacable against terrorism, although he also declared that it was not necessary to combat barbarism with barbarism, a point he repeated in his September speech at the Fortieth General Assembly of the United Nations. Nevertheless the wave of violence continued. Shortly afterward, a *Sendero* "sympathizer" denied any possibility of the PCP-SL holding a dialogue with the government. This rejection was apparently repeated by the exiled relatives of Abimael Guzmán's wife to a top APRA leader visiting Sweden. There was no doubt that *Sendero* had made up its mind regarding its policy toward the new ruling party of Peru. Under these circumstances, Alan García decided to defend his regime the best way he could in order to avoid endangering his "nationalist, democratic, and non-aligned" policies. In 1986 the APRA government decreed a curfew in Metropolitan Lima from 1:00 o'clock to 5:00 o'clock in the morning.

As with the Belaunde adminstration, the main concern of the García government was the generalized violence in almost the entire country, causing thousands of deaths and huge material losses. Together with the escalation of selective killings and widespread bloodletting, Peruvians become more and more uneasy and the number of those who advocated national reconciliation, general amnesty, and dialogue diminished. The most shocking acts of violence during the first year of the new administration were the assassination of the director of the penitentiary El Frontón, the highest political authority of the Department of Ica, and of a Navy rear admiral. With *Sendero* venting its anger on PAP leaders, the PCP-SL joined the ranks of the most rabid and fanatic anti-APRA forces. On 26 May 1986 *Sendero* militants attempted to kidnap Alberto Kitasono, a personal friend of Alan García and PAP's National Secretary of Organization. Four people died in the frustrated attempt.

Sendero's military actions now included the use of car-bombs, the attempt to set a military club in the center of Lima on fire, the killing of Admirals Carlos Ponce Canessa and Gerónimo Cafferata Marazzi and a good number of civilian authorities and judges, armed attacks against the embassies of the USA, the People's Republic of China, and the Soviet Union, and the launching of explosives at factories and PAP district headquarters.

On the other hand, the 19 June 1986 military assault on three Lima and Callao jails seized by rioting *Sendero* prisoners, causing a still undetermined number of deaths (calculated variously from two hundred to three hundred detainees) embarrassed the new administration. It had called in the Armed Forces to restore order in the prisons on June 18, the eve of the opening of the Sixteenth Congress of the Socialist International. *Sendero* responded by declaring June 19 Heroism Day (PCP 1986:94-96). Most of the people, however, continued to support government policy against subversion and terrorism. In the municipal elections of 9 November 1986 the PAP candidates won overwhemingly over the disconcerted conservative and United Left candidates, although the latter obtained about one-third of the votes nationwide. Apparently, the resounding victory of the Apristas and the great popularity of Alan García infuriated *Sendero* to the point of ordering the assassination of PAP leaders, as demonstrated by the killing of César López Silva in front of two of his children. López, PAP's National Secretary of Professional Organizations, was a distinguished 45-year-old physician, trained in the German Federal Republic, who had been president of Peru's Medical Federation.

EVALUATION OF SENDERO

Sendero Luminoso is the most radical movement in the history of Peru. Economic and social reasons, including overpopulation, unemployment, extreme poverty, internal migration, centralization, lowering of the standard of living, increasing external debt, corruption, and so on, have failed to explain satisfactorily this Andean phenomenon. The conceptual approach to the problem perhaps lies in historical and ideological answers as well as in the acute socioeconomic crisis. Although the PCP-SL considers itself Maoist, its strategy more closely resembles those employed by Pol Pot's Khmer Rouge in Cambodia and by the Mau Mau in Kenya than the praxis applied in China by the Communist Party until the Cultural Revolution. Although the PCP-SL considers itself a follower of Mariátegui, other parties that make the same claim deny that *Sendero* is heir to Mariátegui's thoughts[16].

Whatever its true ideology, *Sendero* is capable of recruiting a great number of young people of either sex, especially teenagers, and charging them with dangerous military missions. Although most recruits are of the poorer classes, the PCP-SL has succeeded in gaining the support of some sons and daughters of the middle and upper classes and has even infiltrated the police and the armed forces (Bonner 1988:38). By the end of 1987 the Peruvian government calculated that there were between three thousand and five thousand *Sendero*

---

[16] One of the most eloquent rejections of this claim by Sendero has been given by César Lévano, Secretary General of the Peruvian Communist Party-Majority (Partido Comunista del Perú-Mayoría) (Lévano 1988).

militants and twenty thousand active supporters.

The leaders of the antisubversive war have found the participation of women in terrorist actions to be important, original, ingenious, and disconcerting. They say *Sendero* women are extremely dangerous leaders whose responsibilities include "finishing off" *Sendero* victims. They come from all social classes and regions of the country, especially from the Andean zone. The list of prominent female guerrilla fighters is rather long. In addition to Edith Lagos and Carlota Tello, Laura Zambrano Padilla, ("Comrade Meche") is a well known guerrilla who has been in jail since 1984, accused of numerous terrorist acts. The police confirm the important role of other young women, whom the press calls "the ladies of death," such as the twenty-year-old woman who blew herself up when she attempted to fire a mortar against the convention building of the Hotel Crillón in Lima, where President Alan García was about to open the Sixteenth Congress of the Socialist International. In April 1987 in Lima alone there were 540 women in jails already found guilty of terrorism or awaiting trial, including two foreigners, one from Germany and the other from the United States. Documents captured by the police reveal that between 1983 and 1985 three women had each headed the *Sendero* Political Bureau of Metropolitan Lima: Laura Zambrano (Comrade Meche), Fiorella Montaño (Comrade Lucía), and Margie Clavo Peralta (J. González 1987:81).

Since many of the guerrilla militants are Quechua-phones recruited in areas where the fighting takes place, particularly from the Central and Southern Andean provinces, they have been able to adhere to Mao's guerrilla tactics by displacing themselves in the war theater as fish in the water. *Sendero* has introduced a new type of soldier in Peru, a part-time fighter, who, after the armed action, returns to his or her work in the field or his or her daily chores. Thus the government armed forces are facing an elusive enemy, one not trained in the classical guerrilla tactics of the past to form visible and identifiable moving columns. To this innovation *Sendero* has added assaults on policemen or soldiers, alone or in groups; attacks against military quarters and barracks, commercial establishments, banks, the governing party's locals; and the destruction of bridges, electrical towers, trains, and vehicles of all kinds. What has complicated a more precise evaluation of their armed activities is their policy of not publicizing their acts and not issuing denials of accusations of terrorist acts attributed to them but which appear to have been committed by other groups unrelated to them, including drug traders and plain common criminals. Another curiosity is their policy in their zones of influence, where they allow cultivation of the land only for what is necessary for immediate consumption.

Meanwhile, *Sendero's* military columns, detachments, brigades, and cells continue the bellicose missions which they label people's war. Their militants are loosely spread out to avoid police detection. They are mainly very young. Many are university students, both men and women, or in the upper grades of the secondary schools; there are of course peasants as well who join their ranks. Their specialty is the surprise attack which happens with lightning speed and is very well prepared. They occupy haciendas, attack towns, execute purported enemies, overrun police posts, assault banks, destroy large factories, occupy commercial and government offices, and provide themselves with arms and equipment. They withdraw from their attacks skillfully and swiftly. Their operations are no longer confined to economically depressed areas of the Central Peruvian mountains: they have been extended to other zones of northern and southern Peru, both in the Coast and the Sierra.

Do *Sendero's* tactics represent the expression of a true Pol Pot communism or a Marxism with messianic overtones? *Sendero's* praxis seems to rely on irrationalism and willfulness. Against a historical background of Andean messianism and millenialism, the PCP-SL postulates a *sui generis* interpretation of Marxism-Leninism with the aid of some of Mao's and Mariátegui's thoughts. As passionate devotion to a cause prevails in *Sendero's* general staff, their behavioral pattern points toward the total disruption of the structures of the "formal democracy." Abimael Guzman, well versed in Hegel, adheres to a tripartite structure of the philosophy of history: thesis, antithesis, and synthesis. He and his leaders apparently have concluded that Peruvian conditions demand an emphasis on the second element of this trio. In fact, the ominous development of their actions rests on the belief that in order to arrive at the synthesis, at the apotheosis of their "new democracy," they must resort to the total destruction of the thesis (the present Peruvian reality), applying in their own way the Maoist antithesis used in China during the war against Japan: the scorched-earth tactic. This policy would take the country, according to these ideologues, to the threshold of the world to be constructed.

Abimael and his general staff seem to have chosen to ignore what Heidegger perceived very clearly: that totalist reasoning leads to totalitarian repression, which ends in an apocalyptic holocaust[17].

---

[17] Antonio Cornejo Polar, former president of San Marcos University, remembers Abimael Guzmán as an assiduous reader of Heidegger's works when Cornejo and Guzmán were

Hence, to assert that *Sendero Luminoso* aspires to produce a national holocaust is not an expression of apocalyptic fantasy. There is plenty of evidence that the PCP-SL is carrying out a project to dismantle the present order with the objective of reimposing a new order upon the rubble of the present. The irony is that it has not articulated as yet a coherent and well defined reconstruction plan. If Lenin once said that the most direct revolutionary route to Paris was through Beijing, Comrade Gonzalo leaves no doubt that for him the road to victory over Lima must be initiated in the Andes. If President Gonzalo is taking into account Mariátegui's observation that the greatest reserve of revolutionary energy lies dormant in the soul of the Quechua peasantry, then he has styled himself the great awakener of the Andes.

From the days of Mariátegui, Marxism in Latin America has tended to stress more its spiritual qualities than its materialistic determinism. Ernesto "Che" Guevara's emphasis on the moral reward is but one example. In fact, most of his predecessors and successors have infused their ideology with the supremacy of the will and consciousness over matter. Their writings and speeches have emotional and subliminal bases. Their political vision appears to belong more to the realm of millenarianism than to scientific Marxism. In a sense, they seem to admire Mikael Bakunin's eagerness to transform reality by an effort of the will. They impose on their followers a thorough party integration where the individual merges with the whole. Their spiritualism, of course, is understood by them as a search for the crystallization of ideas by means of a violent revolution to create a better world for the mind and the spirit rather than for the body. In a way, Latin American Marxists, such as Mariátegui, assumed an antipositivist stand, opposed to the capitalistic ethic that emanated from rugged individualism and rampant bourgeois postivism. The extrarational ingredient in their political behavior is their answer to the overstressed rationalization of the positivist frame of mind. Their insistence on revolutionary class and racial collaboration is in direct response to Spencerian positivism that led to the conceptualization of the white superman. Their hope of forging a new humanity lies in the destruction of the present political, economic, and social order. Their final objective is the millenarian hope to turn the existing order on its head. The Peruvian Communist Party known as *Sendero Luminoso* has inherited a great part of this emotional approach to Marxism in order to initiate its apocalyptic ushering in of a new society.

Sendero Luminoso is unique among world revolutionary move-

---

studying at the University of San Agustín in Arequipa.

ments for fusing in its theory and praxis two great myths to which humans respond: the long march and the lost paradise. Moses' crossing of the Red Sea, Mao's classical long march, and Prestes's Column (Hanke 1967:105) illustrate the linear progress toward the domination of man's outer and inner world that *Sendero* pursues. The longing for the reestablishment of the Incan order destroyed by the Conquest is tantamount to the myth of the lost community. In a sense, it is the Andean version of the circular eternal return. *Sendero* apparently aspires to return to the community of wholeness disrupted and alienated first by the *conquistadores* and now by the capitalists. Perhaps the difficulty in legitimizing linear progress of the long march forced *Sendero* to resort to the myth of the paradise lost, which in Peruvian terms is the return to the order envisioned by Andean Messianic tradition dating back from the sixteenth century. This attitude confirmed Marx's observation that when men are about to make a revolution they fortify themselves by acting as though they are restoring a vanquished past.

Abimael Guzmán and his general staff probably embraced Marxism-Leninism-Maoism out of the books and from university teachings. Their conversion was primarily a conscious and rational act, conditioned by voluntarism and a spiritual superstructure. The majority of the rank and file of *Sendero* (particularly among Indians and *mestizos*) took a personal approach to Marxism-Leninism-Maoism and Comrade Gonzalo's ideology. This developed, very likely, through their mythological and spiritualist inclinations. Their belief is ingrained more in their perception of those ideologies, conditioned by their traditional faith in regeneration and in making life more comprehensible and endurable, than on what each theoretician really meant to say. In this sense, Marxism-Leninism-Maoism came to provide the Andean a mystical and mythological vision of regeneration. The religious dimension of Marxism became a belief system capable of mass action of the most unusual type. For *Sendero's* intelligentsia, as for Sorel and Mariátegui, the revolutionary myth would inspire the masses to act as if the myth were true. Thus, in the Andes, as in Russia at the beginning of this century, Marxism has become an energizing myth, a paramount factor in inducing individuals to act in the most heterodox fashion. Therefore, Marxism is understood not as a scientific theory, but as a quasi-religious myth. For them, as for André Malraux, the communist myth gives creative energy to the heroic soul. At the least, we know that Abimael Guzmán learned in his studies of philosophy that Hegelian and Marxist thought have esoteric and mystical backgrounds. Furthermore, Mariátegui taught him that communism is essentially a spiritual movement, and that the force of revolution does not lie in science, but in man's faith, in his passion, in his will, and that "revolutionary movements embody a mystical, religious, spiritual force[18]."

Like St. John's Book of Revelations, the *Senderistas* accept the need for violent confrontation. Their view of regeneration requires that the emergence of a superior human order be preceded by a terrible catastrophe that would destroy the forces of evil. Ironically, Peruvian anarchists and Trotskyists have contributed to *Sendero's* view of secular redemption. The *Senderistas* have aggressively assumed the role of the revolutionaries chosen to usher in the new dawn. They are the chosen: the rest are the damned. Their concept of an ideal society will be forged by the four swords of their tetraideology. For them, *Sendero's* martyrs will make possible the regeneration of the country. Their deeds, no matter how much suffering they bring, are *sine qua non* conditions for their road to victory. They probably are taking into account, consciously or unconsciously, that González Prada said that revolution must be painful in order to be fecund and produce new people: although it spills blood, it creates light; it might submerge men, but it elevates ideas. They probably know that González Prada agreed with Marx in that a revolution is like a childbirth: the more pain it causes, the better the child that is brought into the world[19]. *Sendero* is ready to heed the prophets who predicted cataclysmic violence before the birth of a new humanity. *Sendero's* agenda is a general national conflagration, a holocaust that leads the way toward their millenarian order.

---

[18] For a more extensive explanation of Mariátegui's Marxism, see the chapter on "Religion and Revolution" in my book Poética e ideología en José Carlos Mariátegui (Chang-Rodríguez 1983:83-110).

[19] On González Prada's ideas, see the chapter "Crítica socio-política" ("Sociopolitical Criticism") in Chang-Rodríguez 1957:87-100.

REFERENCES

Arguedas, José María
1956   "Puquio: una cultura en proceso de cambio," *Revista del Museo Nacional* 25:184-232.
1967   "Los mitos quechuas post-hispánicos," *Amaru* 3:14-18

Bonner, Raymond
1988   "Peru's War," *The New Yorker* (4 January 1988):31-58.

Bourricaud, François
1959   "El mito de Inkarrí," *Folklore Americano* 4:178-87.

Chang-Rodríguez, Eugenio
1957   *La literatura política de González Prada, Mariátegui y Haya de la Torre*. México: De Andrea, 1957.
1983   *Poética e ideología en José Carlos Mariátegui*. Madrid: Porrúa Turanzas, 1983.
1987   *Opciones políticas peruanas*. 2nd ed. Trujillo, Peru: Editorial Normas Legales.

Committee to Support the Revolution in Peru
1985   *Revolution in Peru*. Berkeley: The Committee to Support the Revolution in Peru.

Degregori, Carlos Iván
1985   *Sendero Luminoso: los hondos y mortales desencuentros*. Lima: Instituto de Estudios Peruanos.

Favre, Henri
1987   "Perú, Sendero Luminoso y horizontes ocultos," *Cuadernos Americanos* 4 (July-August):29-58.

Flores Galindo, Alberto
1987   *Buscando un inca: identidad y utopía en los Andes*. Lima: Instituto de Apoyo Agrario.

González, Raúl
1982   "Ayacucho: por los caminos de Sendero." *Quehacer* 19 (October):39-77.
1983   "El sendero de Sendero Luminoso," *Debate* 22 (September):24-37.

González, José
1987   "Sendero de mujeres," *Sí* 1.7 (April 6-13):78-85.

González Prada, Manuel
1940   *Anarquía*. Santiago de Chile: Ercilla.
1941   *Prosa menuda*. Buenos Aires: Editorial Imán.

Gorriti Ellenbogen, Gustavo
1984 "Opera de sangre," *Caretas* 814 (August 27):18-19,72.

Granados, Manuel Jesús
1987 "El PCP, Sendero Luminoso: aproximación a su ideología," *Socialismo y Participación* 37 (March):15-36.

Hanke, Lewis
1967 *Modern Latin America: Continent in Ferment. South America.* Vol. 2. Princeton: Van Nostrand Co.

Haya de la Torre, Víctor Raúl
1977 *Obras completas.* 7 vols. Lima: Juan Mejía Baca.

Lévano, César
1988 "Senderos que se bifurcan," *Sí* 47 (January 18-25):22-25.

Macera, Pablo
1984 "Los proyectos nacionales en el Perú," *La República* (January 15):27-30.

Mariátegui, José Carlos
1967 *La organización del proletariado.* Lima: Ediciones Bandera Roja.

Maticorena Estrada, Miguel
1981 "Prólogo." In *Cuerpo político y restitución en Tupac Amaru.* 3rd vol. of the *Colección Documental de Bicentenario de la Revolución.*

McClintock, Cynthia
1983 "Sendero Luminoso: Peru's Maoist Guerrillas," *Problems of Communism* (September-October 1983):19-34.

Mercado U. Rogger
1982 *Algo más sobre Sendero.* Lima: Ediciones de Cultura Popular.
1986 *El Partido Comunista del Perú: Sendero Luminoso.* 3rd ed. Lima: n. p. Emancipadora de Tupac Amaru. Lima.
1987 *El Partido Comunista del Perú: Sendero Luminoso.* 4th ed. corrected and augmented. With an interview with the Maximum Leader Dr. Abimael Guzmán. Lima: n. p., 1987.

Millones, Luis
1964 "Un movimiento nativista del siglo XVI: El Taki Onqoy," *Revista Peruana de Cultura* 3:134-40.

The New York Times, 8 August 1984, p. L5

Ortiz Rescaniere, Alejandro
1970   "El mito de Inkarrí no es un mito," *Educación* 4:34-42.

Ossio A., Juan M., comp.
1973   *Ideología mesiánica del mundo andino.* Lima: Edición de Ignacio Prado Pastor.

Palmer, David Scott
1984   "Rebellion in Rural Peru: The Origins and Evolution of Sendero Luminoso," Paper presented at the National Defense University. Washington, D.C. on April 18, 1984.

Partido Comunista del Perú.
1975   *Retomemos a Mariátegui y reconstruyamos su partido.* Lima: Bandera Roja.
1985   ¡*No votar*! ¡*Desarrollemos la guerra de guerrillas para conquistar el poder para el pueblo*! N. p. Reprinted in *Un Mundo que Ganar* 3 (1985):52-59.
1985 , *Develop Guerrilla Warfare. Don't Vote! Instead, Expand the Guerrilla War to Seize Power for the People!* Berkeley: The Committee to Support the Revolution in Peru.
1986   *Desarrollar la guerra popular sirviendo a la Revolución Mundial.* N. p.: Ediciones Bandera Roja, 1986.

Partido Comunista del Perú, Comisión Política
1968   *Acerca de la historia del Partido Comunista Peruano y de su lucha interna.* N. p.: Ediciones Bandera Roja.

Pedriali, José Antonio
1984   "A guerra de guerrilha na cordillerira peruana: Morote prega a violência revolucionaria." *O Estado de Sao Paulo* 12 February: B1.

Peru, Presidencia de la República
1981   *Perú 1981: Mensaje al Congreso del Presidente de la República Fernando Belaunde Terry.* Lima: Presidencia de la República.

Planas, Pedro
1986   *Los orígenes del APRA: el joven Haya.* Lima: Okura Editores.

Puertas M., Laura
1988   "Asesino saldrá libre," *Caretas* 996 (March 7):36-39.

Reynoso, Oswaldo, Vilma Aguilar e Hildebrando Pérez H.
1979   *Luchas del magisterio: de Mariátegui al SUTEP.* N. p.: Ediciones Narración.

Rojas Samanez, Alvaro
   1985   *Partidos políticos en el Perú: manual y registro.* 4th ed. Lima: Ediciones F & A.

Sánchez, Luis Alberto
   1978   *Apuntes para una bibliografía del APRA: I. Los primeros pasos, 1923-1931.* Lima: Mosca Azul Editores.

Taylor, Lewis
   1983   *Maoism in the Andes: Sendero Luminoso and the Contemporary Guerrilla Movement in Peru.* Working Paper 2. Liverpool: Center for Latin American Studies, University of Liverpool.

Valderrama, Mariano, et al.
   1980   *El APRA: un camino de esperanzas y frustraciones.* Lima: "El Gallo Rojo."